THE EVOLU[...]
HILLARY RODHAM
CLINTON

SQUINT

BRIEF BOOKS FOR A BUSY WORLD
Look More Closely

THE EVOLUTION OF HILLARY RODHAM CLINTON

SONYA HUBER

EYEWEAR PUBLISHING

First published in 2016
by Eyewear Publishing Ltd
Suite 333, 19-21 Crawford Street
Marylebone, London W1H 1PJ
United Kingdom

Typeset with graphic design by Edwin Smet
Clinton picture Gage Skidmore *(Creative Commons license)*
Printed in England by T J International Ltd, Padstow, Cornwall

The right of Sonya Huber to be identified as author of
this work has been asserted in accordance with section 77
of the Copyright, Designs and Patents Act 1988

ISBN 978-1-911335-27-6

The editor has generally followed American spelling and punctuation at
the author's request.

Eyewear wishes to thank Jonathan Wonham for his generous patronage of our press.

WWW.EYEWEARPUBLISHING.COM

CONTENTS

PREFACE

Before writing this book, I had changed my own party from Unaffiliated to Democrat for the purpose of voting for Bernie Sanders in the Connecticut primary. When Okla Elliot, author of *Bernie Sanders: The Essential Guide*, recommended that I write a similar volume on Hillary Clinton, I said no. I wasn't a Clinton booster; I was still bitter about what her husband had done to welfare two decades ago. Then I thought about it for a day and asked myself why exactly I wasn't excited about Hillary Clinton, and the question itself began to snare me. Every reason revealed that I had a gut-level disinterest, though I couldn't say exactly why. This aversion led me to wonder which narratives about her I'd swallowed without even examining them. I decided I wanted to dive in to figure out what Hillary Clinton represents for politics in the United States and in the world at this moment, so I emailed Okla back and said I was in.

Throughout the primary season, the choice for Democrats was framed as simple: Bernie or Hillary, but the urgency propelling the election's tension is the specter of Donald Trump or someone else who's just as bad. Over several months, as I sipped coffee and glanced at the headlines, I'd suddenly be overcome with a wave of fear and turned to my husband or whomever was in the room and asked, "He couldn't *really* be president, could he?" The answer from all corners has gone from laughter to a kind of shrug: well, maybe he could.

Friends – people I've known for years – considered voting for Trump, and some cast ballots for Trump in the Republican primary, as a kind of protest vote, a sort of surrealist Dada performance piece in the voting booth. When pressed, these people say, "Trump is what America deserves," followed by laughter, and the implication that Trump will bring the country to its knees, usher in chaos, and show the nation the ugly face of its own failure against the forces of – what? Hate or mere illogic and reality television? It's hard to say. Other friends found Trump appealing because his mix of positions is such a raspberry to the establishment, and because his lack of seriousness is itself a position about "politics as usual," whatever that might mean to the individual voter. Trump's crafted image of a political outsider reveals one key element about Hillary Clinton's contested image, and the question of whether her political experience and connections qualify or disqualify her for the presidency.

As voters considered their vote for the Democratic primary, the vitriol had reached a fever pitch. Desperation to push for true change in Washington, D.C., unfortunately morphed into a perception that aggressive male Sanders supporters were shaming women who supported Clinton into silence. As someone who was initially mostly interested in the Sanders platform, I read these brief comments online about sexism but didn't feel drawn to delve into them until I began researching Hillary Clinton's current campaign and the questions of whether there were such things as "Bernie bros" who were "mansplaining" the election and thus silencing women who had their own reasons for supporting Clinton. At that point I also needed to better understand what Hillary had done to earn the term "hawk." Clearly, women vociferously supported Sanders, and men supported Clinton. But the current level of feminist discourse and awareness – is this Wave 3.5 or Wave 4? – has played into choices that voters, mostly women, made about their candidate. Hillary Clinton is an anchor point, a concrete representation, for some women about the struggles of women in the United States. She becomes more or less appealing because of the very dynamics of the conversation about her, which I'll discuss. I began to poll friends who were Hillary Clinton supporters in an attempt to understand at the gut level what led them to choose her.

The dynamic itself among the initial candidates shaped each of the candidates' supporter bases in fascinating ways that then affected the general election. In the minds of Trump and Sanders supporters, Hillary Clinton is the quintessential establishment figure: a political name brand, a Washington, D.C. insider, someone who represents the political game as it has always been played. Research into the criticism of Hillary Clinton – mostly arguments in favor of Bernie Sanders – honestly makes me understand exactly why Trump became attractive to many Republican and unaffiliated voters. In other words, I was first very agnostic about Hillary Clinton, thinking that if Bernie Sanders didn't get the nomination, she'd be a safe and non-evil alternative. Then I started reading more about her international connections and, for a moment, I began honestly to understand why Trump was attractive. That was a terrifying moment in and of itself, and it passed with the next breath. But putting myself in the shoes of a Trump supporter, hate for Hillary Clinton is a mix of retrograde sexism and anti-establishment resistance to her domestic and international connections. For Clinton supporters, this reaction clarifies their daily experience: that gender still weighs into every element of one's experience –

which is, to her supporters, part of an argument for why we need a first female president. In short: super-complex, but also interesting.

For Democrats, "electability" – a pragmatic consideration of which candidate might appeal to enough of the voters in order to beat Donald Trump – was a hotly debated question that ended up providing little focus to the primary. But now the Republican Party seems to be moving toward not just business-as-usual but a Claymation-era Heat Miser who imagines the presidency as a kind of Magic Carpet ride to a whites-only utopia. The Republican Party is either self-destructing or turning into a werewolf, and the Democrats are either re-finding their progressive roots in this era of an ever-growing gap between the wealthy and the rest of the country, or they are attempting to keep a steady hand on the shaking, quaking machinery of the government.

And as an interesting side-note, I find that as I've begun the research for this project, I've come to a reassessment of the woman Hillary Clinton is and what she might offer the country. I don't agree with many of her policy recommendations or statements, but the process also leads me to question the extent to which I have absorbed conservative rhetoric as well as sexist assumptions about her that are trumpeted from both the Right and the Left. At the same time, I'm stinging from some of Bill Clinton's policy decisions twenty years ago, and unsure about how much to blame his wife for those decisions. I read three tomes about her life, two written by her. As an unabashed Midwestern nerd who likes the concept of healthcare for all, I couldn't help but begin to feel affection for another woman with those same qualities. All this has made me fascinated with the person Hillary Clinton is as well as the image of her story that has been constructed for the people of the United States.

CHAPTER 1
THE MEANING OF HILLARY

For people in the United States who have been alive and of voting age since the 1990s, looking at Hillary is like staring into a set of angled dressing-room mirrors and seeing images of the United States cast backward into themselves into infinity. Hillary's face represents all of what we want to escape and cannot, or all the hopes we had that were either partially realized or were outright crushed. For a nation without royalty, the idea of familial legacies is both reassuring and suffocating.

For Democrats and those who voted for Democrats in the absence of another viable alternative, the era of Bill Clinton's presidency is partially suffused with nostalgia as the ghost of the Reagan/Bush era was (seemingly) vanquished, the budget was balanced and the economy seemed to turn around, and we were no longer (seemingly) approaching the world with a Cold-War-era "fight-the-commies" mentality. He played the saxophone on *The Arsenio Hall Show*, for Pete's sake. His unofficial campaign song was the bouncy Fleetwood Mac anthem "Don't Stop Thinking About

Tomorrow." He could shake hands with an African-American without oozing hypocrisy. Bill was attractive and dripped charisma in that down-home way, and his wife: she was a real person, a smart woman with a career, and they seemed to have a real partnership. She would do more than choose the White House china. And Hillary made Bill Clinton even more attractive to voters who were looking for an image of a modern family.

But Bill Clinton delivered the country from the Reagan/Bush era with a kind of horrible compromise: the New Democrat. This was Jimmy Carter with brass knuckles, a party that had to get tough to rescue the southern white male vote by promising to enforce a series of belt-tightening bootstrap policies that would end up glorifying the Republican ideals of free trade agreements, destroying welfare, and enacting an era of mass incarceration in the name of a War on Drugs. The New Democrat would roll up his or her sleeves and court corporate donations, and work the bipartisan compromise by any means necessary to inch the country forward instead of backward.

Many progressives in the 2016 primary expressed near-loathing of Hillary, and these same Bernie Sanders' supporters often stumped hard for Barack Obama in 2008. What is confusing, then, is the broad overlap between Hillary Clinton and Barack Obama on so many issues. In fact, Bill Clinton – long said to be right of Hillary – is very similar to President Obama: "Aides on both sides had always maintained there was little daylight between the two presidents on policy."[1] And Bill Clinton's support – and the narrative of continuing the Clinton legacy – helped boost Obama into re-election[2] with the embrace of the "New Democrat" label.[3] So if Obama is so similar to Bill and Hillary is supposed to be Bill's equivalent, if not a little to his left, then why was Obama's election a victory for progressives while Hillary is seen as a complete betrayal of everything progressives stand for?

Hillary has brand recognition because of Bill, which is both her boon and her curse. She is the Coca-Cola to the Pepsi of the Bush family, with an important difference. The Bush money came from oil and family wealth; in contrast, Bill and Hillary have worked in tandem to build a family machine whose wealth emerges from the work of politics itself, from running for office and then speaking and writing about politics.

Daniel Gross describes the combined effort in *Fortune Magazine:*

> Holding and serving in public office
> provides a platform from which they

can monetize experience, connections and prominence. And then they use the wealth gained through, say, speaking engagements and media tours, to lay the groundwork for the next campaign. Electoral office, business, wealth, and public service, all meld together seamlessly.[4]

Gross describes this machine as – even with all the zeros after the figures – something the Clintons have built through their own work: "Democrats are famously the party of labor. So perhaps it is no surprise that their income comes almost entirely from labor – speaking, consulting, and writing."[5]

This is work, of course, but it's working at a job that most people in the United States would never have access to – and the wages of this work include the accrual of power and influence. Hillary received an advance reported at $8 million for her 2003 memoir *Living History,* and $14 million for her 2014 memoir of the Obama era, *Hard Choices.*[6] Bill received a $15 million advance for his memoir, and the Clintons' speaking fees together brought in at least $18 million in 2013 alone, including Hillary's often criticized talks to Wall Street and corporate clients like Goldman Sachs and Fidelity Investments.

This highly effective machine was valued at a combined wealth of $111 million dollars in 2015,[7] and the sources of that money have stirred questions about the potential strings attached to that wealth. But money drives an election fund, and it can be argued that both Bill and Hillary were stumping, writing multi-million-dollar memoirs, and speaking in order to build the next campaign war chest. The Clintons have crafted a political partnership in the public eye in which both partners have become political players. For this reason, among others, Hillary Clinton is saddled with her husband's legacy and his policy decisions; she has benefitted from his connections even as she helped shape his vision.

Hillary Clinton is fascinating as a candidate because of this mystery: to what extent is she an extension of Bill Clinton? Ultimately, figuring out this question gets to the heart of what a long-term marriage or partnership means in an era aiming toward women's equality. To what extent might Hillary have had a role in shaping her husband's opinions over late-night pillow talk and venting sessions? She has always been smart and ambitious; many voters assumed that she was giving Bill advice. But it's impossible ultimately to know how many of her opinions were reflected in his decisions and actions. Feminists recoil at the idea that Hillary might now be seen as merely an appendage of her husband, one who must bear the brunt of his record, while critics on both the left and the right have been gleefully heaping on her plate the implications of her husband's policy decisions.

Hillary seemed intent, however, on standing by her husband even when he messed up as a spouse and a man horrifically and repeatedly along the way, which makes the existence of their marriage and their political partnership something of a miracle. Some assumed that she stood by him not for personal reasons but because of the empire they had built together. Those nuances are unknowable to anyone outside their marriage, however. Many women loathed Bill Clinton and then forgave him because Hillary found a way to survive with him.

Bill and Hillary have alternately stepped forward and stepped back, using both their strengths to support the other, building toward a goal that seems to have been engineered almost from the beginning. And who knows: maybe this was their plan all along, to make Hillary the first female president of the United States.

CHAPTER 2
BEFORE THE "CLINTON":
HER EARLY CAREER

Hillary Rodham was born in Chicago in 1947 and
grew up in Park Ridge, Illinois, a northwest suburb.
She was the eldest of three children, and her father,
a World War II veteran, ran a fabric store. Clinton's
mother, Dorothy Howell Rodham, had a difficult
childhood and left home at age 14; Hillary Clinton
attributes her awareness of child welfare issues
to her mother.[8] Hillary heard Martin Luther King,
Jr., speak in Chicago in 1962, brought to the event
by a church youth group, and describes that as an
influential moment in thinking about social justice.[9]
Hillary campaigned for Republican Barry Goldwater
in 1964 when she was 17, under the influence of her
father, a Republican.[10]

She attended Wellesley College and was
initially active with the Republican group on
campus. After Dr. Martin Luther King, Jr. was
assassinated in April 1968, Clinton helped organize
a two-day strike at Wellesley and worked with the
six African-American students in her class on
concrete demands including "recruiting more black
students and hiring black professors....Eschewing

megaphones and sit-ins, she organized meetings, lectures and seminars, designed to be educational." She commented about these events in an interview in which she claimed that change required more than speeches and demonstrations, but that Dr. King's assassination created a galvanizing sense of change for Clinton.[11] She became a Democrat in 1968.

She wrote her senior thesis on the work of organizer Saul Alinsky, who had written the book *Reveille for Radicals* in 1946. She corresponded with and met Alinsky several times while writing the thesis. Her paper argued that gaining power was the goal of effective activism and "the very essence of life, the dynamo of life," she wrote, quoting Alinsky. She graduated from Wellesley in 1969, then went to Yale Law School, where she met Bill Clinton. In 1971, she lived for a summer in California and interned with the law firm of Treuhaft, Walker, and Bernstein, "known for its radical politics and a client roster that included Black Panthers and other militants."[12] During this summer, she corresponded with Alinsky and asked him when his new book, which would be called *Rules for Radicals,* was coming out. In a letter Clinton wrote to Alinsky, she said that she had "survived law school, slightly bruised, with my belief in and zest for organizing intact."[13] Eventually she developed disagreements with Alinsky's tactics for social change; where he recommended agitation as a way to build public desire for change, she felt the need to work within the system.[14]

She read an article about civil rights lawyer Miriam Wright Edelman's work with the Children's Defense Fund, then went to see her give a speech on campus, where she asked if she could work with the organization.[15] In the summer of 1972, Hillary Rodham traveled to Alabama and visited private schools that were said to cater only to whites after schools had been ordered to desegregate in 1969. Rodham posed as a mother of a new family in town to help determine whether the schools were discriminating based on race. Rodham then worked with the organization in Washington compiling a report. Despite the extensive research, only one or two of these private segregated schools lost their tax-exempt status. She then joined Bill Clinton for the rest of the summer in Austin, where they worked to register voters.[16]

She graduated from Yale Law School with honors in 1973 and then took additional classes at the Yale Child Study Center while waiting for Bill to graduate. In the spring of 1974, she worked as a member of the House Impeachment Inquiry

Staff during the Watergate scandal. She moved to Arkansas with Bill, and they both taught law at the University of Arkansas Law School in Fayetteville. She married Bill in 1975 after he proposed to her in a house he'd secretly purchased. The years after her graduation from law school and settling into life in Arkansas are a whirlwind: in 1976, she worked on Jimmy Carter's presidential campaign, and her husband ran his own first successful campaign and was elected Attorney General of Arkansas. Also that year, she founded the first indigent legal aid clinic in Fayetteville, Arkansas after addressing the House of Delegates to request the funding, convincing them against widespread opposition.[17]

In 1977, Hillary Clinton joined the Rose Law Firm so that there would be a paycheck coming in to supplement Bill's public office salaries. She co-founded Arkansas Advocates for Children and Families, an organization which still exists. Bill was elected governor in 1978 at age 32. Hillary was already focused on her career and on building long-term wealth for the family, along with trying her hand at investment in cattle futures[18] in 1978 to 1979. At the same time, she was appointed by President Jimmy Carter as the first woman to chair the Legal Services Corporation, which provided poor defendants with free legal assistance.[19]

Their daughter Chelsea was born in 1980. The position of governor at this time was a two-year post, so Bill ran again and lost in the same year, and then later regained the position and was governor from 1983 through 1992. Hillary Clinton, meanwhile, brought home the bacon as the first woman to be named full partner at the Rose Law Firm, making more money annually than Bill until they reached the White House. By the time Bill Clinton was elected president, Hillary had a net worth of over $700,000, augmenting her ending salary of $200,000 per year with seats on several boards, including the Arkansas Children's Hospital, the Children's Defense Fund, as well as TCBY, Lafarge, and the Arkansas-based Walmart.[20]

Clinton's seat on Walmart's board in particular has been used as evidence of her pro-corporate leanings, especially as labor activists and women's rights organizations have targeted the corporation for its abuses of workers, its low wages, and its impact on local businesses. She held the seat on that board from 1986 to 1992, overlapping with notorious union-blasting board member John Tate, and apparently did not disagree with any anti-union statements made during taped meetings. I don't know how this record of silence compares to other political leaders who have served on corporate boards. Clinton did, however, push for more environmentally responsible practices and for better treatment of female employees.[21]

Walmart has become the symbol in the U.S. for a reprehensible union-busting corporation that drains money from local businesses. In Arkansas, especially at that time, Walmart was the state's pride and joy, a hometown economic dynamo – and her husband was governor. I imagine Hillary sitting in those meetings and biding her time, wondering what could be said. I have remained silent in important meetings where reprehensible things were said and where I did not have the political capital to object. I understand but might not agree with a situation in which Hilary Clinton, while friendly to unions, might find herself sitting on that board for six years and not picking a fight with the largest employer in the state she called home, not knowing what her husband's political future might bring. Add to this the difficulty that Arkansas is a state with "right-to-work" legislation, a term that sounds great but actually means, in essence, "it's really, really hard to organize a union because we've made it almost illegal."

When Bill Clinton was asked for his view on the matter, he said, "We lived in a state that had a very weak labor movement, where I always had the endorsement of the labor movement because I did what I could do to make it stronger. She knew there was no way she could change that, not with it headquartered in Arkansas, and she agreed to serve."[22]

In other words, Hillary Clinton sat on a corporate board in a dicey political situation in the mid-eighties. She spoke up enough that founder Sam Walton called her "a very strong-willed young woman," she's still having to answer for it 25 years after she left the board, and the final word on the coverage from ABC News comes from her husband, who is allowed to let her off the hook. While I am myself a strong union advocate and activist, I've bought stuff at Walmart. Labor – or any other political fight – doesn't win points through purity contests. I find the argument about Clinton's lack of pro-union sloganeering during Walmart board meetings to be not a very compelling one. It's a fact that gets repeated again and again, either because it's a catchy sound bite or because discussion of the real concerns about Hillary's reliability for labor – from her support for anti-labor education "reform" or her off-and-on support for free-trade agreements that impact U.S. workers – is more difficult to explain in 30 seconds.

As they packed up their Arkansas home and prepared to move to Washington DC, the scrutiny for the Clintons was just beginning, and Hillary had already begun an unintentional campaign of her own, compiling a political resume of offhand remarks, careful statements, and strong political positions that would be scrutinized for the rest of her life.

CHAPTER 3
HILLARY WAS RIGHT ABOUT HEALTHCARE, AND WE HATE HER FOR IT

In 1993, Hillary Clinton became the First Lady of the United States, though her political role during her husband Bill Clinton's presidency has sometimes led her to be called "co-president" in both laudatory and disparaging terms. Bill Clinton ran partially on a platform to reform health insurance in the country, and after he was elected he launched almost immediately into drafting the Health Security Act, which included a requirement that employers provide healthcare to all their employees. Bill Clinton appointed Hillary as the chair of the Task Force on National Healthcare Reform. Seizing on her visible role in the developing plan, opponents quickly dubbed the proposal "Hillarycare."

In much of the coverage about the healthcare plan, Hillary Clinton is often portrayed as its mastermind and thus as being too pushy and overestimating her ability to craft this complicated legislation. In reality, while she was definitely smart and articulate enough to explain policy, she was not present at any of the organizational meetings in which the goals of the policy were composed, according to Paul Starr, co-founder of *The American Prospect,* who was drawn into discussions about the Health Security Act based on writing and research he had done on healthcare. Instead, Hillary's job was to travel and to speak to citizens, explaining the plan. In the process, she became the public face of the legislation, which included speaking stops where the Secret Service required her to wear a bulletproof vest and where she was sometimes met with organized, screaming counter-protestors incited by right-wing radio.[23] Starr writes,

> The overall direction of policy was not Hillary's choice. She had not been present at the key meetings during the campaign when Clinton had discussed health policy with his advisors, and in the first days in the White House, she was just familiarizing herself with the approach to reform that her husband had adopted.[24]

Starr states that challenges with the plan emerged immediately, as Bill Clinton got into legal trouble for appointing his First Lady to head a Task Force when that wasn't the normal way of doing things.

Several working groups convened to deal with the nitty-gritty of the possible legislation, but interest groups and the press complained that they didn't have enough access to those conversations, dubbing them "secretive." Ball-park projections and initial notes were leaked to the press, resulting in a front page article in the May 3, 1993 *The New York Times* entitled "Health-Care Costs May Be Increased $100 Billion a Year."

President Clinton wanted the rough outline of the plan to move quickly, but the budget stood in a deadlock that year, with all other legislation stalled behind it. Starr writes that President Clinton had initially been fine with a compromise plan involving managed care, but "tacked left" in 1993 to include a prescription benefit for Medicare recipients, hoping to make good on another of his campaign promises. Looking back, President Clinton said he should have held back the legislation at that point, especially after a grim budget discussion: "I set the Congress up for failure."[25] The truth of partisan politics was much more complex, and it involved an overlap between insurance-industry organizations aggressively opposed to any changes to their profit and far-right Republicans dredging up any possible scandal to stonewall the kind of social change that would prove their agenda disastrously misguided and to avoid giving Clinton an easy re-election.

After the "catastrophic" midterm elections "in which Republicans, led by Newt Gingrich, won the House for the first time in 40 years," Hillary was widely blamed for the healthcare plan and thus for the entire move rightward in the country. Lawrence O'Donnell, former aid to Senator Patrick Moynihan, was quoted by Carl Bernstein as saying, "My view is Hillary Clinton destroyed the Democratic Party."[26] Starr writes that, although an article by James Fallows in the January 1995 *Atlantic* refuted the popular claims about the supposed secretive nightmare of the Clinton proposal, Hillary's role continued to live on in statements repeated in other *Atlantic* articles and in Carl Bernstein's biography of Hillary Clinton, and so too did the idea that the legislation failed "because of her secretiveness and rigidity."[27] It's amazing, really – the evil power that this narrative has given her. It wasn't profit interests that derailed healthcare reform: it was a woman.

In her memoir *Living History,* Clinton writes that she was able to contain herself until a gathering with her female staffers: "Now it all came out. Fighting back tears, my voice cracking, I poured out apologies. I was sorry if I had let everyone down and contributed to our losses. It wouldn't happen again. I told them I was considering withdrawing from active political and policy work, mainly because I didn't want to be a hindrance to my husband's Administration." Then each woman at the gathering told her exactly why she couldn't give up: because the country needed her.[28]

The implications for Hillary Clinton as a politician with regard to healthcare and public perception are twofold. First, there's the fear that she will be forever associated with a smear campaign that implied that she was controlling and manipulative, pulling the strings behind the curtain. Second, there's the real impact that this legislative failure might have had upon her own method of proceeding as a legislator, making her much more cautious than she might otherwise have been. In the aftermath, "shattered, Hillary threw herself into her husband's strategy of triangulation, a word she uses approvingly in her own memoir, *Living History*."[29]

Clinton did not retreat to the extent that she failed to take future advocacy opportunities. Melanne Verveer, her former chief of staff, said that in the aftermath of the healthcare failure, "Hillary pleaded with her husband to expand the coverage for children, which he did through the State Children's Health Insurance Program, passed in 1997."[30] Hillary worked with Teddy Kennedy and Orrin Hatch on a bipartisan effort that expanded healthcare coverage for low-income children at a time during Clinton's second term when the President and his Cabinet wanted to distance themselves from the healthcare battle.[31] Starr believes Hillary took the blame for her husband's healthcare policy, but that her past work with children's health could lead her to turn a "State Children's Health Insurance Program into the foundation of universal health coverage for children" and a way to "give Americans confidence that their government could guarantee health care for all."[32]

The larger question, a game of "what if," is whether we would currently have the Affordable Care Act without Hillary Clinton. It's likely that her long-term concern for health must have played into Bill's formulation of his opening gambit to revise the healthcare system in the United States during his first term. The template that President Obama used to craft the Affordable Care Act was very similar to the one she ran on in the 2008 primary. And when he announced to his cabinet early on that he was planning to launch his own healthcare effort, cabinet members were divided and noncommittal until Hillary stepped up in a meeting and threw her considerable reputation on the issue behind him. As a result, Obama was able to go to the public with the support of his administration.[33]

What this means for her potential actions as president with regard to healthcare is unclear, though she has vowed to defend the Affordable Care Act and go after "predatory pricing" of unaffordable pharmaceuticals.[34] Starr writes,

> The general tenor of her rhetoric is consensus-oriented – and necessarily so, given the highly polarized public perceptions of her history on the issue. Surely one political lesson from the earlier struggle is to frame a proposal that creates the broadest possible support for reform and splits the opposition.... More than any other candidate, she has to set achievable goals in health care – and, if elected, achieve them[35].

When I graduated college in 1993, Hillary was just beginning to stump for healthcare, and I took note with a mix of surprise and admiration that a First Lady was so deeply engaged in essential policy. I believe that even though a segment of the population was not inclined to look favorably on efforts to change healthcare, Bill Clinton's reliance – or dependence – on his wife, and his support of her role in touting the policy, ended up cementing her in at least part of the public's mind as a leader, redefining what the role of the First Lady might entail as well as what she might be capable of in the future. Whatever else the Clintons have going on in their complicated relationship, it is clear that the mix includes his respect for her leadership abilities and intellectual gifts. And it's clear, beginning with this first major challenge, that she could weather the storms of controversy and intensely personal and often sexist criticism, drawing on sources of internal strength, re-assessing, and managing to stay engaged in the issues she cares about.

The failure of their healthcare effort had other causes and other effects. Way back twenty-odd years ago, there was a scary squishy red-faced man yelling into microphones about how he should be king of the world and how poor people were evil. You might call him proto-Trump, but his name was Newt Gingrich, and if you've never heard of him, you should look him up, because he matters. After Republicans swept the House in 1994, Republican Speaker of the House Newt Gingrich introduced a "Contract with America," a kind of Republican manifesto that included proposals for sweeping tax cuts and changes to welfare. He mentioned that children of moms on welfare should be placed into orphanages, among other wacko ideas.

People worried that Gingrich was amping up to be our next president. At the end of 1995, Republicans sent Bill Clinton two versions of their federal budget, with huge cuts to basic social services. Republicans threatened to shut down the government if they did not get their demands, and then carried through, closing all federal services except the most basic on November 13, 1995 and remaining shuttered for six days. Bill crafted his own version of a budget, consulting Hillary in particular on strategies to save Medicare and Medicaid. And then he decided he had to roll up his sleeves and make some deals.

CHAPTER 4
BILL CLINTON SOLD US OUT, AND HILLARY WAVED US GOODBYE, PART I

If you say the word "Clinton" in the United States, many progressives and liberals see red; they are reacting to two bills signed not by Hillary Clinton but by her husband 20 years before the 2016 election. The first was the "Violent Crime Control Act" of 1994, and the second was the "Personal Responsibility and Work Opportunity Act" of 1996.

With these two laws, Bill Clinton seemed to be morphing the values of the Democratic Party and turning them ultra-Republican. This is all relevant for Hillary Clinton today, because she must either continue with, or reject, this legacy. Hillary Clinton did not sign either of these pieces of legislation, but she endorsed them. In the case of the welfare bill, she threw her weight as a child advocate behind it, helping to round up votes for its passage.

Michelle Alexander writes in *The Nation*: [Bill] Clinton was the standard-bearer for the New Democrats, a group that firmly believed the only way to win back the millions of white voters in the South who had defected to the Republican Party was to adopt the right-wing narrative that black communities ought to be disciplined with harsh punishment rather than coddled with welfare. Reagan had won the presidency by dog-whistling to poor and working-class whites with coded racial appeals: railing against 'welfare queens' and criminal 'predators' and condemning 'big government.' Clinton aimed to win them back, vowing that he would never permit any Republican to be perceived as tougher on crime than he.[36]

The Violent Crime Control and Law Enforcement Act of 1994 included the "three-strikes" sentencing (doling out life sentences for those convicted of a violent crime after two prior convictions) that many criminal justice experts believe led to the unprecedentedly high levels of incarceration in the United States as well as billions of dollars in funding for prisons. Interestingly, Vice President Joe Biden wrote the bill, and Clinton's rival Bernie Sanders voted for it.

Alexander writes that "both Clintons now express regret for the crime bill," which had far-reaching effects:

By the end of Clinton's presidency, more than half of working-age African-American men in many large urban areas were saddled with criminal records and subject to legalized discrimination in employment, housing, access to education, and basic public benefits – relegated to a permanent second-class status eerily reminiscent of Jim Crow. It is difficult to overstate the damage that's been done. Generations have been lost to the prison system; countless families have been torn apart or rendered homeless; and a school-to-prison pipeline has been born that shuttles young people from their decrepit, underfunded schools to brand-new high-tech prisons.[37]

In 1994 Hillary "used racially coded rhetoric to cast black children as animals" when describing her support for the crime bill: "They are not just gangs of kids anymore,' she said. 'They are often the kinds of kids that are called 'super-predators.' No conscience, no empathy. We can talk about why they ended up that way, but first we have to bring them to heel.'"[38] Although she discusses the controversy over the welfare bill in her memoir *Living History,* Hillary does not make mention of the crime bill

— which could be taken as an indication that she was less involved with this legislation. After being challenged by activists at a fundraiser about her use of these terms, she apologized. [39]

In the 2016 campaign, Hillary Clinton is calling for an "end to the era of mass incarcerations," a major change from her 2008 position embracing mandatory minimum sentencing.[40] She announced that she would stop accepting donations from private prison firms.[41] Her website also describes a "plan to ban racial profiling, eliminate the sentencing disparities between crack and cocaine, and abolish private prisons, among other measures."[42]

CHAPTER 5
BILL CLINTON SOLD US OUT, AND HILLARY WAVED US GOODBYE, PART II

Bill Clinton signed onto a Republican-driven effort and effectively destroyed the New Deal-era safety net of welfare in 1996. But he wasn't just a victim; he promised in his campaign that he would "end welfare as we have come to know it," and he did. The "Personal Responsibility and Work Opportunity Act" replaced a successful cash-based program called Aid to Families with Dependents and Children (AFDC) and turned it into Temporary Assistance for Needy Families (TANF). This changed how funding would be distributed: rather than a coordinated federal program, money would now be doled out to the states in the form of "block grants." The guidelines going along with these block grants were vague, so states could determine how to distribute their welfare benefits with little federal oversight or enforcement. Because these grants turned a comprehensive program into a series of dollar signs, it then became easy to cut, and the amount of money doled out in those grants was frozen.

In *Living History* Hillary writes, "I agreed that the system was broken and needed to be fixed, but I was adamant that whatever reform we advocated would ensure an adequate safety net for individuals to move from welfare to work. I expressed my opinions vigorously and often to my husband as well as to his staff members charged with shaping reform." She said she would publicly oppose any "caving in to a mean-spirited Republican bill that was harmful to women and children."[43] At the same time, she expressed concern about "welfare-dependent Americans" and advocates for work rather than welfare.[44]

Bill Clinton vetoed two Republican welfare bills, which included such harsh stipulations as cutting food stamps and ending welfare to legal immigrants along with full freedom for each state to decide whether to offer any welfare benefits at all. According to Bill, Hillary "prodded him to use his veto pen when he was eager to cut the best deal possible with a newly elected GOP-controlled House under Speaker Newt Gingrich."[45] Bill Clinton added that, when she reviewed the welfare bill, "she said, 'You can't sign this, you can't block-grant food stamps or medical care, and I think there's not nearly enough money for transportation and child care in it.'" But in the end, according to Bill

Clinton's account, they both supported it "to deny the GOP a potent wedge issue in Clinton's 1996 reelection campaign."[46]

As of 2013, only 26 percent of poor families with children were enrolled in TANF, "compared to 74 percent before reform went into effect."[47] In the first few years after the law's passage, poverty actually went down and workplace participating went up, because the economy was doing well, but then things started to turn very bad. Looking at the long-term effects of this program, *The Nation* cites a paper by the National Poverty Center which says that "extreme poverty" has increased sharply between 1996 and 2011; extreme poverty is defined "using a World Bank metric of global poverty" by counting those people who survive on less than $2 a day. The undertone is chilling: we need to use a World Bank metric meant for developing nations, many struck with famine and civil war, to capture the extent of need in the United States.

Right before the law went into effect in 1996, about 636,000 households were estimated to be at this extremely low cash income level of $2 per person per day. By 2011, there were 1.65 million households (with 3.55 million children) living in this situation. This represents an increase of 159 percent of people living in dire poverty;

the report says this impact is seen "particularly among those most impacted by the 1996 welfare reform." Accounting for Earned Income Credit and other non-cash benefits (such as food and housing assistance) reduces this figure by up to 68 percent, so some have argued the levels of poverty are not as bad overall – but these non-cash forms of assistance still do not raise anyone above the poverty line. The study estimated that two causes of this rise in extreme poverty were welfare reform and the 2008 Recession.[48]

Bill Clinton was a Democrat, so what was he thinking? And why does this matter to Hillary in 2016? The underlying vision championed by Bill Clinton was the idea that he was not merely a Democrat but instead a "New Democrat," and that term helps explain both the reasons for his legislative agenda and the discomfort that many traditional liberals and progressives have with the Clintons. The "New Democratic" vision involved a canny or tragic (depending on who you ask) absorption of elements of the conservative agenda, including the larger turn toward neoliberalism. Decades later, people in the United States still worry that they can't trust the degree to which the Clintons' agenda will be a betrayal of traditional Democratic interests and programs.

"Neoliberalism" is a vague concept that stretches far beyond the Clintons; the term is confusing because it sounds like "liberal," which in the United States is today a moderate progressive. But here the term refers to economics. Neoliberals believe that the market – if it functions efficiently and budgets are balanced – will take care of people all on its own, without need for social programs. One element of neoliberalism important for the issue of welfare is the idea of "restructuring," which typically involves cutting spending on social programs. Often these cuts are linked to the idea that poor people need to be taught to live better; the unfair assumption is that they are poor not because of unequal opportunity and wealth distribution but because they are not making the choices that would make them richer.

An economist named Milton Friedman claimed that trying to redistribute wealth would lead to totalitarianism, and this notion was very influential with Cold-War era conservative thinkers like Ronald Reagan in the United States and Margaret Thatcher in the United Kingdom.[49] The 1980s were an era of backlash against gains made by various social movements in the 1960s and 1970s. The weird thing – and a fundamental problem for the left in the United States and beyond – is that the Democratic Party has been consistently neoliberal since the Reagan era, often settling for small gains or basically the same foreign policy as the Republicans while letting these terms about social programs frame the debate. Some say it is because elections are so expensive and Democrats know they need to court corporate donors to fund them,[50] so they have to use the conservative language.

Some might say that in 1996, Bill Clinton was using this neoliberal legislation to ensure his re-election for a second term. The question, then, is the extent to which Hillary Clinton really supported the law and the extent to which she did so "grudgingly," as Michelle Goldberg describes, "after her attempt to create a universal health insurance program was blamed for the disastrous 1994 midterms."[51]

In the same year the law passed, Hillary Clinton published her book, *It Takes a Village,* which advocated that children thrive when the whole community looks out for their well-being.[52] She describes the desire to write the book as emerging in opposition to Newt Gingrich's view of dealing with poverty in the United States, along with his proposal that the children of women on welfare be put into orphanages. She writes,

After spending years worrying about how to protect and nurture children, now I feared that political extremism could sentence the poor and vulnerable to a Dickensian future. Although it wasn't political in a partisan sense, I wanted my book to describe a vision different from the uncompassionate, elitist, and unrealistic views emanating from Capitol Hill.[53]

Her sentiments were important, but many critics saw irony in the contrast between her ideals and the concrete effects the welfare legislation would have on children in low-income families. Hillary Clinton had described Miriam Wright Edelman as a mentor and a woman who shaped the direction of her career. To Wright Edelman, the welfare reform legislation represented a major break in her friendship with Hillary Clinton, and she called it "an abomination."[54]

After the law was passed, members of Clinton's administration quit in protest, including Peter Edelman, the husband of Hillary Clinton's mentor Miriam Wright Edelman, who founded the Children's Defense Fund. Hillary Clinton described the resignations as "principled decisions, which I accepted and even admired," but felt she had crossed the line from advocate to politician and hoped that welfare reform would put the debate to rest and allow the country to address other elements of poverty and its causes. She described the law as "a historic opportunity to change a system oriented toward dependence to one that encouraged independence," but also a "far from perfect" law representing a "pragmatic" decision that avoided handing the Republicans a "potential political windfall."[55]

The question for me, and for many, is the extent to which Hillary Clinton believes the right-wing language she sometimes employs. Ultimately, if she uses the language, she's responsible for its implications, despite whatever triangulation maneuver she's trying to employ. Feminist scholar Johanna Brenner describes the post-Reagan era of middle-class feminists who:

> embraced the idea of self-sufficiency through paid work, even though it was quite obvious that the low-paid precarious jobs open to so many single mothers would never pay a living wage, that the childcare stipends provided (to the poorest women) were inadequate for quality childcare, and that after-school programs for older children were unaffordable[56].

This group of women – not all feminists, and not all Second-Wave feminists, but mostly among the professional class like Clinton – aimed to "uplift and regulate those who come to be defined as problematic – the poor, the unhealthy, the culturally unfit, the sexually deviant, the ill-educated."[57]

It's clear that Hillary Clinton is a fan of work as a means of uplift, which indicates that she doesn't always understand the implications of policy on the lives of poor women. In 2002, as New York Senator, Hillary Clinton supported then-President George W. Bush's proposal for tougher work requirements for welfare recipients, which she describes as a negotiation to get $8 billion in childcare funding and a "vast improvement" over Bush's original bill.[58]

The implications of this strategic move rippled beyond the deal itself, according to progressive critics, who claimed, "She is perceived as a progressive Democrat, and so she is giving cover to other Democrats to do the wrong thing."[59] She supported the legislation by saying that those who were on welfare "are no longer deadbeats – they're actually out there being productive."[60] The term "deadbeat" vastly oversimplifies the challenges of living in poverty, including the systemic structures that make rising into the middle class more difficult than a personal choice to work. For low-income mothers in particular, the cost of childcare is usually higher than the wage earned in a low-paying job, making the choice to be working for no money while away from one's children a fool's dilemma. The idea that caring for one's children – or other sick or disabled members of one's family – is not "productive" highlights one of the ways in which Hillary Clinton was not thinking of the feminist implications of her statement. And in her 2003 memoir *Living History,* Clinton was still supporting the work requirements in the 1996 welfare legislation: "I didn't think it was fair that one single mother improvised to find child care and got up early every day to get to work while another stayed home and relied on welfare."[61] As late as 2008, she was still calling the 1996 welfare legislation successful.[62]

Part of the greater concern among progressives is the extent to which Clinton is willing to use right-wing language to make incremental changes in bad legislation and the extent to which she believes the New Democrat neoliberal rhetoric that imposes punitive restrictions on the poor without investigating the full implications.

Interestingly or strangely, the 2016 HillaryClinton.com website does not have an issue tab for "welfare." Instead, some of her positions can be found under "economy," where she includes feminist rhetoric: "For too long, issues like equal pay, paid leave, and affordable child care have been put off to the side as 'women's issues.' Hillary believes they are crucial to our competitiveness and growth – and to lifting incomes for working families."

Her plan for paid family leave would be funded with a tax on the incomes of those making above $250,000 a year. She supported a bill to create a national affordable housing trust fund in 2003.[63] In 2000, she adopted a "New Agenda for a New Decade" that included

> expanding the Earned Income Tax Credit, increasing the supply of affordable child care, reforming tax policies that hurt working families, making sure absent parents live up to their financial obligations, promoting access to home ownership and other wealth-building assets, and refocusing other social policies on the new goal of rewarding work, we can create a new progressive guarantee: No American family with a full-time worker will live in poverty.[64]

One of the difficult and potentially punitive elements of that 2000 plan is the focus on child support from absent parents, which is vastly more difficult – if not impossible – for unemployed or underemployed parents, and which can lead to more struggling and absent parents becoming involved in the criminal justice system.

Progressives and liberals wonder what deals Hillary Clinton might cut in order to ensure her own future elections; but as always, she's clearly savvy in reframing her issues. Ultimately, the question of her rhetoric and her arguments will have huge implications on how the debate over contested entitlement programs proceeds in the United States. With the release of her 2014 memoir *Hard Choices,* she references a new respect for admitting mistakes. The question is whether this reflects a confidence in her ability to provide leadership rather than merely to react to and contain the agenda of the extreme Right. And as the Trump candidacy shows, this extreme and extremely fragmented Right Wing in the United States remains a force to be reckoned with.

CHAPTER 6
OVARIAN OFFICE

Hillary Clinton has been compared to many female leaders around the world as people try to make sense of the idea of a woman's being in charge. In some ways, the wide reach of these comparisons is a little offensive, as the main criteria – political prominence and a uterus – seem to in and of themselves make an argument for more women in politics. The comparisons are also a blunt instrument; inviting a comparison between conservative former British Prime Minister Margaret Thatcher and Hillary Clinton tends to associate the two together, though they might not be otherwise linked in terms of style or politics. And our gender politics are not yet at the stage where we might meaningfully compare Hillary to a man for purposes other than denigration. Who are her real buddies across the gender continuum, and who are her appropriate comparisons?

1. Aung San Suu Kyi: Clinton is fast friends with the Burmese democratic reformer and put in a great deal of energy during her tenure as Secretary of State to assist with the transition to democracy in Burma.

2. Margaret Thatcher: Mark Penn, campaign manager for Hillary in 2008, thought he'd tried to mold Clinton's public image to that of Thatcher and her "toughness."[65] This was a cynical attempt to defend against fears that a woman might be too mushy for politics, and it failed. So how much *is* Clinton like Thatcher? Well, some argue that she *is* Thatcher, or a continuation of her. Doug Henwood writes in *The Nation*, "The Clintonites purged the Democrats of their social-democratic wing, consolidating the victories of the Reagan Revolution."[66] Under that logic, you could argue that Hillary is Margaret Thatcher-lite. But in another way I am suspicious of this claim. Would anyone call Barack Obama Reagan-lite? No. The very idea galls.

Because so few women have been in power, the idea of comparison to those who have held major political office leads one to wonder whether Hillary Clinton would be "another Thatcher" if not a progressive savior. But Sarah Ditum promotes an interesting antidote to this fear in *The New Statesman:*

> Women do not deserve to exercise power only on the condition that we would do it 'better' than men and promote the feminist cause. Women have the right to political

office exactly as men do, and that means that we can do it well or badly, feministly or unfeministly – just as men have been doing for millennia. Women are entitled to be wrong and mediocre sometimes. Being wrong and mediocre is part of the human condition, and women are allegedly human. At the despatch box or in the boardroom, we should have our fair share because it's simply a matter of justice. Until we have our fair share, we have no idea how the normalising of female power might change the world; but we don't have to change the world to merit our half of it.[67]

3. Angela Merkel of Germany: Hillary and Angela are buddies. Hillary says,

Well, I have to say that I highly admire Angela Merkel. I've known Angela since the 1990s, she and I actually appeared on a German TV show together. I have spent personal time with her. She is, I think, a really effective strong leader and really right now the major leader in Europe, not just in Germany. I admire her political skills and her principles, her strong work ethic. I just find her to be an incredibly important person in the world today and I look to her to see how she's managed it.[68]

In 2011 a German paper, *The Frankfurter Allgemeine*, ran a picture of the two of them standing side by side in their pants suits with their hands clasped and with their heads cropped out, asking readers to guess who was who. Merkel gave Clinton a framed copy of the paper. [69]

4. Mother Teresa: the two were friends – but they had an open beef about abortion! Clinton says,

> Mother Teresa was unerringly direct. She disagreed with my views on a woman's right to choose and told me so. Over the years, she sent me dozens of notes and messages with the same gentle entreaty....I had the greatest respect for her opposition to abortion, but I believe that it is dangerous to give any state the power to enforce criminal penalties against women and doctors.
> I consider that a slippery slope to state control of reproduction..."[70]

I think, personally, it's pretty tough to take a consistent stand against Mother Teresa.

5. Claire Underwood, from the Netflix series *House of Cards*: Claire Underwood seems less

Clinton and more Lady Macbeth, though *House of Cards* creator Lord Dobbs says Hillary is the character's real-life counterpart, and he's fascinated by the role her history plays in her current campaign: "That baggage is her strength but also her vulnerability. We just have to wait and see where the balance lies on that. Though it is bizarre that the system that was bred out of [rejection of a King] has produced the Bushes, the Kennedys, the Clintons, the Roosevelts...."[71]

6. RuPaul: Famous musician and drag queen who endorsed Hillary Clinton with a tweet: "You better work, @HillaryClinton!" Both, it might be argued, have had to perfect the art of the flawless image.

7. Jackie Kennedy: Hillary asked Jackie for style advice, as she reports in *Living History,* and was put at ease when Jackie told her to find her own style and not worry about the critics.

8. Eleanor Roosevelt: Hillary's imaginary BFF. When she got depressed after a political low point, her staff made a photo collage of Eleanor standing next to a young Hillary in order to perk her up.

9. Michelle Obama: Hillary said in her book *Hard Choices* that things were tense initially but warmed up after her friendship with Barack improved during her tenure as Secretary of State. Michelle Obama confidently told campaign staffers during the 2008 campaign that Hillary *wouldn't know what hit her* with the Obama campaign.

10. Eva Perón: Some saw Hillary's campaign posters used in the South and Southwest in Fall 2015 as a visual reference to posters for the musical *Evita*, which chronicled the life of Eva Perón, an actress who became first lady of Argentina. Perón and her husband were socialists.[72] The posters are nice, but Hillary evoking socialism in any form seems disingenuous, though I would welcome any such campaign announcement.

11. Berta Cacéras: A Honduran environmental and indigenous rights activist, Cacéras founded the Council of Indigenous People of Honduras and was awarded the Goldman Environmental Prize. She was assassinated in March 2016, a week after she voiced her opposition to a proposed dam in the Gualcarque River Basin, funded by financial backers from around the globe. Over 100 activists have been killed in Honduras since the coup of

2009, which Hillary Clinton as Secretary of State did not designate a military coup and which led to the current repressive government.[73]

12. Jill Stein: Stein was the Green Party Candidate for President in 2016, and she calls Hillary Clinton the candidate of Oligarchy. Stein is a physician who calls for "a Green New Deal, calling for a transition to 100-percent clean and renewable energy by 2030, and investing in public transit, sustainable agriculture and conservation, thereby creating new jobs."[74]

CHAPTER 7
HILLARY IS A WOMAN, AND
THAT'S APPARENTLY A PROBLEM

For many, Hillary Clinton's presidential run represents the potential shattering of the ultimate glass ceiling, an image she was reluctant to play on in her 2008 bid for the Democratic nomination but which she mentioned in her concession speech after Barack Obama received the Democratic Party nomination. She thanked the 18,000 million supporters for helping her making "18,000 million cracks" in the glass ceiling. In 2016 she launched a campaign less influenced by her husband's campaign advisors and their concern with her "toughness" and more influenced by her whole identity, which includes her particular attachment to issues facing women and girls both in the United States and around the world.[75] Clinton herself was reluctant to run on the basis of her gender because gender itself promises nothing with respect to policy when it comes to politics (and opponents are quick to bring up the case of the UK's Margaret Thatcher to make this point). Supporters put forth the idea that Hillary's grace under pressure is itself an advertisement for her political competence.

The evolving role that sexism has played in the campaign – and in her supporters' and detractors' views of Hillary and her abilities – has been a constantly moving target. Plenty of journalists have been chided for the media's long-standing obsession with her hair instead of her political contributions.[76] At the same time, Republicans vying for their party's nomination have been roundly mocked for their likeness to Grandpa Munster from the sitcom *The Munsters* (Ted Cruz) and their hair and tiny hands (Trump). The sexism, then, comes into play because such mocking of physical attributes does not automatically reflect upon a man's perceived ability to govern. However, with a woman, physical attributes immediately act as an argument against her intellect, supporting a pre-conceived notion of incompetence.

The Right Wing in the U.S. has had twenty five years to mold the public's perceptions of Hillary, as Chez Pazienza writes: "Hillary Clinton's reputation is largely the result of a quarter century of visceral GOP hatred." Pazienza writes that the Republicans have been working on this portrait consistently, so that even liberals have this impression as their go-to:

Hillary ... has always been cast as an arrogant bitch, a soulless *bête noire*, an irredeemably corrupt and fundamentally dishonest political hustler. From the very beginning of her time in the national political limelight, she was vilified for refusing to simply sit back and be an ornament on the White House Christmas tree, as she was apparently supposed to. And when she ventured out into her own separate political career, what was considered calculating but somehow forgivable from her husband became merely calculating – and nefariously so – from her. Bill was allowed to be Slick Willy. Hillary was just rotten to the core.[77]

From "Travelgate" to "Filegate" to "Whitewater," the Right Wing has spent enormous time and energy connecting her to various concocted scandals, even going so far as to imply that the Clintons' friend Vince Foster – a close advisor who committed suicide shortly after the beginning of Bill Clinton's first presidency partially as a result of these smear campaigns – was somehow killed by Hillary in an elaborate cover-up of her misdeeds.

Pazienza's clear statement gave me pause: "if you're a liberal who believes these things about

Clinton – if you see her as anything other than a liberal Democrat who's guilty of nothing more than being a politician with faults and with a plethora of enemies like every other on this planet, including Bernie Sanders – you've proven that the protracted smear campaign against this woman has worked. You prove that the GOP won a long time ago."

I think some of my own gut-level unease about her would fall into this category.

She's been mocked because of her laugh, which is often described as a "cackle."[78] When she got too angry in the congressional hearings regarding the Benghazi attack in January 2013, the *New York Post* ran the headline, "No Wonder Bill's Afraid," and said she "explodes with rage."[79] Like all women, Hillary's actions are viewed as constantly in need of editorial direction from men. After her primary wins in mid-March 2016, MSNBC commentator Joe Scarborough tweeted on March 15, 2016, "Smile. You just had a big night."[80] For many women, Scarborough's comment echoed street harassers who routinely tell women to "Smile!" as a way of getting a reaction and putting a woman off balance.

She described the conscious crafting of her own now-muted delivery in her 2003 memoir *Living History:* "I had learned during health care reform that my own strong feelings rarely help me in my delivery of a public address. Now I had to make sure that the tone or pitch of my voice would not confuse the message. Like it or not, women are always subject to criticism if they show too much feeling in public."[81]

Some female supporters explain their support of Hillary's campaign on the basis of identification; they've been through a similar grueling series of evaluations in the workplace, constantly unable to prove their worth to men and having to work twice as hard. Hillary Clinton has been under constant international scrutiny for decades, sometimes under such pressure that her continued involvement in politics is astounding. Many supporters cite her over-qualification for the job of President, linking the scrutiny to the idea that sexism drives those who constantly undervalue Hillary Clinton's record. As Joan Walsh writes in *The Nation*, "I really don't want to see her abused again. I'm tired of seeing her confronted by entitled men weighing in on her personal honesty and likability, treating the most admired woman in the world like a woman who's applying to be his secretary."[82] Hana Schank writes in *Salon* that this identification hits home with women who are old enough to have experienced "chronic, internalized, institutional sexism" in the workplace over decades.[83] Goldberg seconds this analysis, connecting it to Clinton supporters' understanding of Clinton's less-than-ideal policy positions in the past:

> Supporting Clinton means justifying the thousands of concessions she's made to the world as it is, rather than as we want it to be. Doing this is easier, I think, when you are older, and have made more concessions yourself. Indeed, sometimes it feels like to defend Clinton is to defend middle age itself, with all its attenuated expectations and reminders of the uselessness of hindsight.[84]

The additional complication in the case of Hillary is the question of "likability," a no-win game for women in the public eye who are engaged in politics. Her ambition, which would be a mere requirement in a male candidate, is often regarded as pathological.[85] She has less overt charisma than Bill Clinton – though perhaps 99.9% of the world population falls into that category – and because she's so associated with her husband, she seems to fail by comparison. In some ineffable way she is a kind of political Yoko Ono, a blank template on which men (and women) can project every negative motive and trait. Hillary Clinton didn't break up the Beatles, of course...or did she?

The amorphous and utterly subjective quality of likability is potentially freighted with sexist judgment. Hillary loses on this count because she's serious about her job, so she's characterized as an earnest nerd or policy wonk. Ironically, she is reviled for having to work twice as hard as a man to prove her record and her competence. To some degree, this is the anti-intellectualism that dogs debate in the United States; Al Gore had to deal with similar repeated diatribes against his wonkishness, but "the fact that Clinton is the first woman to have a conceivable chance of winning the presidency gives the contempt with which she is treated an extra sting."[86]

A popular meme that circulated again and again on social media in early 2016 featured two side-by-side headshots of Hillary and her Democratic primary opponent Bernie Sanders under the heading, "Bernie or Hillary? Be informed. Compare them on the issues that matter." Below their photos, the issues of concern included topics such as Radiohead, *Star Wars*, or *Harry Potter* among many others. Hillary's purported response was over-the-top clueless, as in the *Star Wars* image in which her position was supposedly "makes 'Live Long and Prosper' hand signal," thus joking that she'd be clueless enough to confuse *Star Trek* with *Star Wars*. Bernie's fictitious responses were on-point and current, as detailed as any hipster would require, and Hillary's were "pandering and robotic."[87] Whereas Bernie Sanders freely admits he was "not a good student,"[88] Hillary Clinton couldn't help but graduate with honors. Clinton is a good girl: *Parks and Recreation's* Leslie Knope with her binders but without the self-deprecating goofiness, the Tracy Flick character from the movie *Election* – in so many of our stories about women, the good girl is devious, cold, and deserves to be taken down a notch to learn her lesson. The issue of wanting the presidency too much, having too much ambition, is itself seen as a problem, as Bernie Sanders' campaign manager Jeff Weaver implied in April 2016 by saying that Clinton would "destroy the Democratic party" to "satisfy the secretary's ambitions to become President."[89]

The good girl is too earnest and can never be the cool dude. Keli Goff writes in the *Daily Beast*:

> The real problem for Hillary Clinton is not that her husband is more likable than she is, but that it is obvious that she cares so much – like a lot of women do...women are

taught early on to spend much of our time, energy and social capital pleasing others. Boys are taught to be smart. Girls are taught to be smart – but not at the expense of being popular, and certainly not at the expense of being pretty. Because after all, accomplishments ultimately mean very little in the big scheme of things if when it's all said and done you're a woman who is perceived as unattractive, unlovable and unlikable.[90]

Reviewing the range of reactions to Hillary Clinton over the decades, it's clear that she's made many adjustments to her image as a way to counter public criticism – and each of those adjustments seemed to be wrong. Initially, she was perceived as too far left and too outspoken: "before she was excoriated as a sellout corporatist, she was excoriated as a feminist radical."[91] Michelle Goldberg sums up the confluence of Hillary's persona and her policy positions in *Slate:*

It's understandable that, after all she's been through, Clinton has a hard time being frank and open with voters. But it's still a problem, for her and for those of us who want her to win. Part of what's so frustrating about being a leftish Clinton supporter is that much of what her progressive critics say about her is true. She's a hawk. She spoke in favor of welfare reform during her husband's presidency. She believes Wall Street has a significant role to play in the economy. She's cautious and calculating."[92]

Calculation and caution often get read as coldness, another criticism with sexist implications. The issue of "excitement" extended to coverage of her campaign and her supporters in a self-enforcing loop. Anna March writes in *Salon* that the enthusiasm of Bernie Sanders' supporters received more media attention than Clinton's:

The popular media seems more interested in covering how 'exciting' the campaign of Bernie Sanders is.... Does the media really mean young, mostly white people's excitement? After all, white men don't run the table anymore. Excitement over Hillary's support from groups as varied as Planned Parenthood, workers' unions, LGBTQ rights groups and disability rights advocates is downplayed."[93]

Likability connects to several other similarly amorphous qualities that influence and form public perceptions of a candidate. One of these issues is the overriding sense that Hillary Clinton is not trustworthy. Her tenure as Secretary of State has been riddled with questions about her email accounts and her actions with regard to the bombing in Benghazi. In its endorsement of her campaign, *Rolling Stone Magazine* describes this as "the lingering haze of coordinated GOP smear campaigns against the Clintons...which after seven GOP-led congressional investigations has turned up zilch."[94] It's likely that the trustworthiness issue is also related to concerns about her and her husband's real estate investments (the Whitewater affair, rooted in a bad investment that Republicans dug into for years with no indictment, at a cost to taxpayers of over $70 million) as well as the Clinton Foundation and their financial ties (which I will address later). However, Keli Goff writes, "The even larger question, however, is why so many voters have such strong negative reactions to Hillary Clinton in the first place. After all, many of the same voters who disdain her for being 'dishonest' will cheer for her husband. You know the one who actually did lie to all of us."[95]

Bernie Sanders took Hillary to task for claiming she has "evolved" on issues, implying that her changing positions make her unreliable.[96]

Politicians evolve and change their positions over time, especially those who have been in the public eye as long as Hillary. She has finessed the descriptions of some of her positions, from abortion to gun rights, and outright changed others, such as on marriage equality and trade agreements. She has also apologized for mistaken positions, which is a refreshing behavior for a political candidate. However, no one should assume that when a politician speaks – especially a politician with such a long history – that they are simply speaking the truth about how they feel. Positions are crafted based on strategic goals and alliances.

Hillary has been called a "shape-shifter" – which sounds much more fundamentally evil than a flip-flopper, almost a kind of demonic possession – and any association with her brands one as evil by association. The term is obviously used as an effort to dehumanize her, and it implies that she is a fundamentally untrustworthy being, someone whose essence is shaped around the tendency to lie.

As feminist political scientist Jocelyn Boryczka would say, Hillary Clinton along with all women can be conceived of as a "suspect citizen." Boryczka writes that women are conceived of as "moral guardians" who "can be perceived as failing to uphold their civic obligation to carry the double burden of moral responsibility for preserving the nation's common good." When women step outside of the hearth and home, they are breaking an implicit rule, therefore are by nature untrustworthy: "Mistrust confers a level of illegitimacy that places women's citizenship under suspicion, making them vulnerable to societal blame for events such as political decay well beyond their control and even to charges that they are traitors, outlaws, and, on occasion, terrorists." [97]

Under Boryczka's framework, attacks against Hillary's humanity or virtue in particular can be seen as a backlash against feminism: "Assigning women the double burden of moral responsibility for self, family, and the nation equates any real or perceived failure to fulfill their civic obligations with traitorous behavior and triggers backlash politics." [98] While this does not at all exempt women from criticism, it requires us to examine the degree to which perceived unreliability snowballs into a sexist caricature in which Hillary is inhuman or evil.

What we know based on her positions is that Hillary *has* evolved: from Republican teen to moderate left-wing young woman to "New

Democrat" to however she'd define herself now. Scott Lemieux writes in a piece titled "Hillary Clinton has evolved since the '90s. You probably have too" that a politician's change in position has to do with responsiveness to his or her base, which is something we *want* in a politician: "A party's leaders tend to move with their parties. To assume the Hillary Clinton of 1994 would be an accurate reflection of the Hillary Clinton of 2017 is to fundamentally misunderstand how politics works."[99]

Hillary is also much more cautious and circumspect, based upon decades of public scrutiny and attack. In some ways, the underlying concern among Bernie Sanders supporters about her tacking positions has to do with concern that her orientation toward caution and consensus will prevent her from acting as the leading edge for a changing and obviously left-leaning Democratic Party. Vice President Joe Biden, who did not endorse a Democratic Candidate during the primaries, seemed drawn to the soaring rhetoric and positions of Bernie Sanders. Biden said, "I don't think any Democrat's won saying 'We can't think that big – we ought to really downsize here because it's not realistic.'"[100] Many took this statement as an implicit criticism of Hillary and fears that her consensus-seeking would be about compromise with Republicans at the expense of leadership.

Though Clinton is often accused of being untrustworthy with regard to statements in her current campaign, fact-checking research into her statements reveals her to be "the most honest of the bunch" including her Democratic primary rival Bernie Sanders.[101] Jill Abramson, a journalist who has covered the Clintons over the years, says Clinton is "fundamentally honest and trustworthy" and that the perception of her being untrustworthy comes partially from Hillary's desire to have a "'zone of privacy' that she protects too fiercely." Abramson adds analysis from Colin Diersing of Harvard's Institute of Politics, who believes "a gender-related double standard" is applied to Clinton; he writes, "We expect purity from women candidates."[102]

On the issue of trust, and in other ways, Hillary Clinton is saddled with public perceptions about her husband's presidency, and the question of whether she is actually a separate person from Bill Clinton is yet another element of sexism that connects with her husband's political record and that ties into millennia of women's fight for the basic right to have autonomy and control over their own lives. At the same time, part of her argument for her own political resume includes her years as First Lady, which means she brings her husband's legislation along with her in a more formal way than might otherwise be the case. We can ask the question of whether she would be running for President without Bill Clinton and her years as First Lady, and the answer would probably be no. Hillary depended on Bill to get to this phase in her political career, but at the same time, many have wondered whether Bill Clinton would have cinched the presidency without Hillary working behind the scenes supporting him.

The Clinton power-couple evokes another suspicion of powerful women in relationships, which is that the woman must be a tyrant pulling the strings (another Yoko element). In the early years of the twenty-first century, it's still almost impossible for many people to truly imagine a marriage in which two intellectual equals discuss major personal and workplace decisions, support each other, and use both partners' contributions to build a whole greater than the sum of its parts. Because many cannot imagine this – or because the reality terrifies – many resort to the default notion that seems to preserve the image of a male's traditional autonomy: Hillary must have devoured

Bill's soul, and has been walking around inside his skin like a body snatcher.

The larger dilemma with regard to these sentiments is that – even if they are sexist, they translate into politicos' analyses and voters' behaviors. While the measure of "electability" is partially a game for pollsters, it is also an issue freely used to argue against Hillary's candidacy. Some polls run during the primary season that favored Bernie Sanders' candidacy measured likability rather than electability, with likability connecting to subjective characteristics, such as which candidate seems more trustworthy.[103]

Electability played a key role in voters' debates regarding a match-up between a New Democrat and a democratic socialist, with the winner to face-off against Donald Trump, an issue that continued to provoke crisis for voters. *Rolling Stone* endorsed Hillary Clinton because of her "experience, the ability to enact progressive change, and the issue of who can win the general election," though the magazine has also run articles critical of her.[104]

If Hillary is elected president of the United States in 2016, she has much to gain from abandoning the constricting elements of the 1990s "New Democrat" formulation as well as the carapace she's developed to shield herself from criticism. It remains to be seen whether she sets her sights higher than merely maintaining the existing Clinton legacy and forges her own path by embracing her inner Yoko Ono, and listening and learning from the political agendas of her constituents.

When I polled my friends and read commentary about the 2016 primary, it became clear that undecided Democrats might have swung toward Hillary not because of either candidates' stance on the issues but because of the conduct of the other candidates' supporters. Joan Walsh writes in *The Nation*,

> When I've disclosed that my daughter works for Clinton – in *The Nation*, on MSNBC, and on social media – we've both come in for trolling so vile it's made me not merely defensive of her. It's forced me to recognize how little society respects the passion of the many young women – and men – who are putting their souls into electing the first female president.

Heated political debate is nothing new, especially among those who feel they are battling for the soul of a political party. In the 2016 primary, Bernie

Sanders was seen by many of his supporters as the last opportunity to redeem the Democratic Party from its corrupt ties to Wall Street, the last chance to right the ship that otherwise seemed headed for the whirlwind of climate destruction, widening gaps between the haves and have-nots, and militarized conflict. And in a battle posed as life or death, Hillary was posed as the false savior, the "more-of-the-same" candidate who would not turn the wheel far enough to avert disaster but instead dupe middle-of-the-road-supporters with her lies. The argument against Hillary was an opportunity for leftists to engage with the nature of liberalism. In this process, the harsh terms of debate may have turned potential Bernie supporters toward Hillary, especially because it's difficult for all involved to see when scorn for a political position becomes condescension for a candidate's supporter. As Joan Walsh wrote during the primaries, "I'm sick of the way so many Sanders supporters, most of them men, feel absolutely no compunction to see things through female Clinton supporters' eyes."[105]

There were arguments against so-called "Bernie Bros," or young male supporters of Bernie Sanders who felt compelled to "mansplain" the entire election, assuming that a female Hillary supporter has chosen that candidate out of ignorance.[106] Others said the "Bernie Bro" epithet applied to a few bad apples who happened to be most visible because they were demographically more likely to be actively engaged on social media.

Walsh writes that the consequences of the flame wars weren't considered by Sanders' supporters because Hillary supporters were seen, as women often are, as an endlessly pliable resource who would forgive all if their candidate loses: "Of course we won't do that; we're women! We're trained to think about everybody else's needs first. It's not just that: women will be hurt the most by a GOP presidency."[107] Some Bernie Sanders supporters, on the other hand, said they would not vote for Hillary even when she won the nomination.

When I posted an invitation on social media asking any Hillary supporters to send me messages with their reasons for choosing her in the primaries, they responded in droves, and quickly. Many prefaced this with an apology of sorts or a request for anonymity: "I wouldn't say this online..." or "I've been hesitant to be public about this," citing feared pressure from friends. In the call for comments, I specifically asked friends not to post on my Facebook wall because I didn't want a senseless argument, and yet a long string of pro-Bernie comments began from my male friends. For a moment, and then more than a moment, I began to see what these Hillary supporters were saying. These tiny annoyances of a few Bernie supporters online would hardly have steered my own selection of candidate. But the larger issue is that these small slices of behavior echo my entire life experience as a woman. That's almost enough for a woman to say, as one of my friends did, "I'm more with Bernie on economic issues. But as a woman, I'm with Hillary."

Supporters see their public support for her not only as an attempt to elect a candidate but also, in Sady Doyle's words, as

> a way, however small, to start shifting the cultural dialogue, to allow for a world where women aren't suffocated or crushed by our expectations of them – a world where Hillary, and every future female president or presidential candidate, can focus on the tasks at hand, and not have to climb over a barbed-wire fence of hatred in order to change the world.[108]

CHAPTER 8
IS HILLARY A FEMINIST?

While it's true that a female president would represent an historic first for the United States and would have a clear, global, symbolic impact, the conversation around women's rights and feminism has evolved beyond the idea that a person with a uterus would automatically be the best candidate for women.

Former U.S. Secretary of State Madeline Albright introduced Hillary Clinton at a campaign event in New Hampshire in February 2016 by saying that there was a "special place in hell for women who don't help each other."[109] The semi-threatening tone turned off many who don't want to feel that support for Hillary is owed just because she's a woman. Albright's statement was part of what led commentator Maureen Dowd to write a piece for the *New York Times* entitled "When Hillary Clinton Killed Feminism," which also argues that Clinton's out-of-touch campaign evinces an individualistic air of the presidency's being owed to Clinton.[110] This, according to Dowd, was further injury after Albright, Gloria Steinem,[111] and Hillary Clinton killed "institutional feminism" in the 1990s by failing to come to Monica Lewinsky's defense.

What's painful about this statement is that it also evokes a sore spot in Hillary Clinton's marriage: the number of times she has denounced any woman who may have been the victim of her husband's sexual advances. Carl Bernstein's biography of Clinton, *A Woman in Charge,* describes Hillary Clinton's "aggressive" campaign to discredit Gennifer Flowers after she came forward with revelations about her affair with Bill Clinton as well as Hillary's efforts to get women to "sign statements in which they were supposed to say they'd had no relationship with him; Hillary also made disparaging remarks about Monica Lewinsky.[112] Conor Friedersdorf writes in *The Atlantic* that without "minimizing any unfairness experienced by her husband's sex partners or alleged victims, it seems to me that asking a man or woman to react rationally *and* sympathetically to a person just as they're revealed to be having an affair with their spouse, or accusing their spouse of a crime, is to demand superhuman self-control and circumspection."[113] To be fair, Hillary was also enraged at her husband. She writes in photo captions in *Living History* of a photo taken after the Lewinsky scandal broke, "The last thing I wanted to do was to go on vacation with Bill Clinton." And in another, "I'd believed him. Why he deceived me is his own story, and he needs to tell it in his own way."[114]

Hillary was also criticized for acting as the defense attorney in a 1975 rape case in which the victim was a 12-year-old girl. She asked to be removed from the case, but when she was not, she admitted finding loopholes to get the plaintiff's sentence reduced.[115] On tapes of the discussion, she is heard laughing about a polygraph test her client passed and saying that it forever destroyed her faith in polygraphs; conservative pundits removed this context to claim that Hillary Clinton was laughing at a rape victim.

Hillary Clinton has not always supported women, and she doesn't actually seem to demand that women support her. Clinton is not telling her supporters she is owed the presidency (though her supporters may believe she is). The assumption that a woman would support Hillary merely because she's a woman, no matter what her positions on other issues, would seem to be particularly outmoded[116] when viewed through the lens of intersectional feminism – a term coined by Kimberlé Crenshaw in 1989 to express the awareness that women experience oppression in varying configurations and in varying degrees of intensity"[117] complicated by race, class, sexual and gender orientation, among other life experiences.

In her 2016 campaign, Clinton gave special attention to the issues of poor women and women of color, using the language[118] of intersectionality to describe how race, gender, poverty and other social forces come together in a situation like the tainted public water of Flint, Michigan in February 2016. Clinton says she does not expect women to vote for her merely because she's a woman, as she has spent her life working for women to have more choices.[119]

On the bedrock feminist issue of Lesbian-Gay-Bisexual-Transgender Rights and free choice, however, Clinton has a rockier history. Clinton had what *The Economist* described as a "farcically late conversion" on the issue of marriage rights.[120] She also has the baggage that her husband signed the 1996 Defense of Marriage Act, which defined marriage as that between a man and a woman, and that she herself did not take a position against DOMA for years.

Hillary Clinton is a visible figure at the global level in advocacy for women's rights, and she is known for a 1995 speech in Beijing to the United Nation's Fourth World Conference on Women that is seen as a "watershed moment in the history of the global women's rights movement" in which she said, "Women's rights are human rights."[121] As

Secretary of State, she integrated women's issues into her work in many countries and advocated for Security Council 1888, requiring the UN to protect women and children from sexual violence during war.[122] During her time as Secretary of State, she made women's rights a key agenda item, including in Afghanistan, where the life expectancy for women jumped from 44 to 62 between 2001 and 2012.[123]

Hillary is often described as a liberal feminist, but it can also be argued that she has changed her politics over her long career in response to pressure and changing eras. It's common shorthand to lump all Second Wave feminists under the umbrella of "liberal," but feminist scholar Johanna Brenner describes "social-welfare feminists" in the United States as those who

> look to an expansive and activist state to address the problems of working women, to ease the burden of the double day, to improve women's and especially mothers' position in the labor market, to provide public services that socialize the labor of care, and to expand social responsibility for care (e.g., through paid parenting leave and stipends for women who care for disabled family members).[124]

In many ways, this was Hillary Clinton's initial agenda in the 1970s up through her attempts to put healthcare reform front and center in the 1990s. Domestically Clinton has been active as an advocate for equal pay for women. She co-sponsored the 2009 Lily Ledbetter Fair Pay Act, which expanded workers' abilities to take pay discrimination cases to court, and had co-sponsored previous attempts to get this legislation passed.[125] She advocated for the Bush administration to look into and document the existence of a gender wage gap.

However, her husband pioneered the "New Democrat" model, and by many accounts she situated herself to the left of him but then was either subsumed or volunteered to move into the professional class and adopt the agenda of liberal feminism. This was during the era of neoliberalism, which Brenner defines as "the political context for the successful backlash against the radical demands of feminists, anti-racist activists, indigenous peoples, and others." As one staffer describes Clinton: "she invests very heavily in American progressivism as a younger woman," the staffer adds, "and it sort of hangs her out to dry."[126]

The Clintons arrived in the White House to end a twenty-four-year span of Republican rule in the United States, interrupted only by Jimmy Carter's presidency of 1977-1981. To win a second term, Bill Clinton made several deals with the devil, adopting the language of "capitalist restructuring" in the form of dismantling welfare, which meant that, in Brenner's words, "second-wave social welfare feminism was not so much co-opted as it was politically marginalized."[127]

One question to ask is the extent to which Hillary Clinton's life story is not about the decisions she made but the history she endured and the way in which she may have adapted her language to changing tides and contexts beyond her control. She cannot ever be considered radical, as she seeks not social upheaval in the U.S. but rather the opposite approach of spreading the American model across the globe.

For some who identify as feminists, Clinton's economic policies may not promise enough change for women in the lower and middle classes. Some have called Hillary Clinton a "boardroom liberal," primarily because she is deeply entrenched in capitalism and the belief that open markets create the conditions for social change and open societies.[128] However, the description of the boardroom liberal quoted above views social movements as "nagging impediments," whereas Hillary Clinton has repeatedly stated her support for movements as the key to pressuring for change from outside the system – while she works from the inside. Still, she invokes the language of the market as a change agent often enough that activists are not entirely sure whether she is reliable in support of social justice causes.

CHAPTER 9
HILLARY HAS RICH FRIENDS, IS RICH

The Clintons together have a lot of money, though their fortunes have risen and fallen over time as they've solicited donors and spent millions on campaigns. Though the wealth itself might lead Hillary Clinton to be out of touch with the lives of middle- and working-class voters, deeper concerns include the degree to which donors' agendas would consciously or unconsciously shape Clinton's domestic and international agenda and her policy decisions – though Hillary on occasion has shown the ability to oppose the will of her donors on environmental and other issues.

How much money do the Clintons have, and where is it?

When Bill Clinton left office, Hillary's net worth was at negative $8 million due to legal bills racked up by the Whitewater and Monica Lewinsky investigations. "Whitewater" refers to a real estate investment that Hillary and Bill made while he was governor of Arkansas; Republicans have tried for years to make the investment seem like a massive conspiracy rather than an accounting mess and money-pit created by a shady business associate, and all the effort has done is waste time and smear Hillary (but somehow not Bill, magically, as tends to happen) with the vague sense of financial impropriety without turning up any evidence.

Since then, however, Hillary's net worth has swollen to $31 million or more. She donated the proceeds of her book *It Takes a Village* to charity, but she made about $10 million from her book *Living History.* The Clintons own homes in Washington D.C. and in Chappaqua, NY, but those seem to be in Bill Clinton's name because they don't show up on her financial statements.[129] Other investigations show that Clinton's worth increased by $10 million in 2009 without a discernible cause. Then in 2011, her total net worth dropped from $30 million to $13 million, which might have been caused by transferring money to her husband or placing it in a "blind trust." Then in 2014, she raised $12 million from speaking fees. Estimates place the Clintons' combined wealth at around $111 million.[130]

Then there is the Clinton Family Foundation. The Clintons have donated millions of their own money to charity – about $15 million between 2007 and 2014 – which means tax write-offs. But 98% of that money went to their own foundation, which they use for travel and to pay their staff.[131]

The foundation "now includes 11 major initiatives, focused on issues as divergent as crop yields in Africa, earthquake relief in Haiti and the cost of AIDS drugs worldwide. In all, the Clintons' constellation of related charities has raised $2 billion, employs more than 2,000 people and has a combined annual budget of more than $223 million."[132] The foundation's finances have gotten messy for the Clintons and have raised eyebrows, especially after the couple was required to release the donor lists when Hillary became Secretary of State and the international network of the Clintons' friends began to make people wonder how friendship and favoritism influenced policy:

> Today, the Clinton Foundation is unlike anything else in the history of the nation and, perhaps, the world: It is a global philanthropic empire run by a former U.S. president and closely affiliated with a potential future president, with the audacious goal of solving some of the world's most vexing problems by bringing together the wealthiest, glitziest and most powerful people from every part of the planet.[133]

Where did the Clintons get this money? Much of it comes from donors. The Clintons have a huge operation devoted to fundraising for elections and causes, and they have cultivated their donor lists since Bill was governor of Arkansas. Bernie Sanders criticized Hillary Clinton for her fundraising practices, including a huge fundraiser hosted by George Clooney; what goes unremarked upon is that President Barack Obama held a similar Clooney fundraiser in May 2012.[134] Obama had originally been critical of Super-PACs, but turned to fundraising events with them in 2014.[135] This might be the result of his drawing closer to the Clintons and their fundraising machine after Bill Clinton stepped in as a highly visible figure during Obama's re-election campaign.

While many donors are individuals with an interest in politics, some have corporate ties, and some have international ties (which I discuss in my section on international politics). Lobbying and corporate donations are such a presence in the United States that this might be the central reason that Clinton has been hammered for her ties to Wall Street. She received speaking fees of $675,000 for three talks to Goldman Sachs as well as fees from many other financial institutions. [136] Although she's been asked, she refuses to release the transcripts of the speeches to Goldman Sachs, which makes her look like she has something to hide. One commentator imagines:

> My guess is that in the speeches, Clinton acknowledges her various friends and acquaintances at Goldman Sachs (and other Wall Street firms) and praises them for the work they are doing. 'You guys get a bad rap but ....' Yes, it's standard-issue small talk. But it could look really, really bad in the context of the campaign.[137]

The cause-and-effect of donation to legislation is "often fuzzy," says Jill Abramson, who adds that investigative articles end up with no clear ties though raising questions: "It was bad judgment, as she has said, to use a private email server. It was colossally stupid to take those hefty speaking fees, but not corrupt. There are no instances I know of where Clinton was doing the bidding of a donor or benefactor."[138] *The Wall Street Journal* tried to draw a connection between favors supposedly done to UBS bank and donations from UBS to the Clinton Foundation, but it is difficult to prove a cause-and-effect relationship.[139]

The real critique of the entwinement between Wall Street and Washington goes much, much deeper than speaking fees. As one example,

Robert Rubin, a former partner at Goldman Sachs, "has played an inordinately important role in Washington," including heading up the National Economic Council created by President Bill Clinton and then as Treasury secretary.[140] Robert Hormats is another USB employee who was sworn in as Under-Secretary for Economic, Energy, and Agricultural Affairs in 2009.[141] These guys are mostly economists, but come on: how could they not have mixed loyalties? The revolving door between Wall Street, lobbying, and government creates an insider corporate culture. Hillary Clinton did not create this situation, but critics worry that she will unquestioningly continue to use advisors with strong Wall Street ties to shape the economy.

Probably the best analysis I've seen of the overlap between Clinton's finances and her politics comes from Naomi Klein's essay in *The Nation*, "The Problem with Hillary Clinton isn't Just Her Corporate Cash. It's Her Corporate Worldview." In this piece, rather than casting vague aspersions, Klein hones in on Clinton's method of doing politics by persuading rich people to donate to charitable causes, or "philanthrocapitalism." As Klein explains: "The problem with Clinton World is structural. It's the way in which these profoundly enmeshed relationships – lubricated by the exchange of money, favors, status, and media attention – shape what gets proposed as policy in the first place."[142] While sucking up to corporate donors might be merely a slow or ineffective way to get things done, it is suicidally slow when it comes to confronting the issue of climate change, which requires massive changes, urgency, and pissing off and controlling multinational energy corporations who are used to running roughshod over humanity. More on this in the section on environment, including Hillary's occasional record of opposing her wealthy donors. But this issue of philanthrocapitalism gets at the heart of the issue, rather than trying to pin Clinton via guilt-by-association.

Voters are justifiably enraged by the state of the U.S. economy, and in particular by the lack of real follow-through after the subprime mortgage crisis of 2008 that touched off a recession that impacted the lives of many. This issue is on top of the massive widening of the gap between the most wealthy and the rest of the nation as well as the wage stagnation that sparked the Occupy Wall Street movement of 2011. Voters are not stupid: they see the connection between their disappearing standard of living and the Wall Street bankers sucking income into sheer profit and waste. They want action.

Where does Hillary Clinton stand with regard to Wall Street? First, apparently, we must go to her husband. Some argue that the chaos sparked by banks that morphed into behemoths that were judged "too big to fail" was created by bills signed during Bill Clinton's presidency.[143] Bill Clinton signed a bill into law that repealed elements of the Glass-Steagall Act, a Depression-era law that prohibited financial institutions from consolidating different functions. However, most economists argue that decades of financial deregulation during previous Republican presidencies had pretty much rendered the law "toothless."[144]

She gave speeches in 2007 – a year before the 2008 market crash – about subprime mortgages, calling them "a serious problem affecting our housing market and millions of hard-working families." She provided a range of possible solutions including "expanding the role of the Federal Housing Administration, more borrowing options for underprivileged and first-time homebuyers, more safeguards against predatory lending practices and policies intended to prevent foreclosures"[145] and sponsored a bill with these solutions in 2007. She then released a six-point plan[146] in March 2008 for increased financial regulation, which upset some of her Wall Street donors.

In her 2008 campaign, she "positioned herself as the populist candidate to the left of Barack Obama on several economic issues, angering some of her Wall Street donors and winning her broad support among organized labor and working-class voters," according to the *New York Times*.[147] However, this article presents the analysis that Clinton is no longer seen as an advocate on economic issues because once she became Secretary of State, she was out of the domestic loop in the following four years, when Senator Elizabeth Warren took her place as the domestic advocate for working people and Clinton became more associated with her husband's centrist legacy.

The extent to which Clinton is compared to Elizabeth Warren is interesting: "Robert B. Reich, a secretary of labor during the Clinton administration who has advised Mrs. Clinton's campaign, said the comparison with Ms. Warren 'personalizes it far too much. This is a broad-based movement to take back our democracy and make the economy work for everybody instead of a small group at the top,' he said."[148] It's almost as if there's no way for voters to get around the anti-feminist narrative of pitting one woman against another.

Hillary Clinton's current plan for Wall Street involves "a 'risk fee' for banks over a certain size. Instead of automatic consequences for too-large banks, however, Hillary's plan would empower regulators to take action. Under Clinton's plan, large firms would be required to break apart, but only if they could not demonstrate that the can be "managed effectively."[149] In other words, it sounds like the onus would be on regulators to go to battle with these large firms and prove individually that each one is problematic.

Her campaign website states that she will "tackle dangerous risks in the financial sector" and "appoint and empower tough, independent regulators and prosecute individuals and firms when they commit fraud or other criminal wrongdoing." Another position on the same page is to put an end to "quarterly capitalism" and "revamp the capital gains tax to reward farsighted investments that create jobs" as well as "reform executive compensation to better align the interests of executives with long-term value."[150]

Economist Thomas Piketty writes in *The Guardian* in February 2016 that he sees little chance of Hillary Clinton altering the structure of income tax, which he argues is one of the drivers of income disparity in the US.[151] He explains that the tax rate "applicable to the highest incomes" was reduced to 28% during the tax reform of 1986 (otherwise known as *Reagan-Era Hell*; my words, not Picketty's) and remained frozen at around 40% since then. Between 1930 and 1980, the average tax rate on this income bracket was 80%. He describes Hillary Clinton as having more progressive economic suggestions in her last presidential run, but that she now seems to be "defending the status quo, just another heiress of the Reagan-Clinton-Obama political regime."[152]

Hillary Clinton is seeking to banish that impression by offering more specific domestic economic proposals. On April 5, 2015, Clinton stood as major supporter of New York state's $15-an-hour minimum wage law, the first passed in the nation – beating California by an hour,[153] while standing by a lower commitment of $12 an hour for a federal minimum wage law, with $15 for fast-food, childcare, and home-care workers.

CHAPTER 10
HILLARY IS A CAPITALIST

One of the biggest critiques of Hillary, from a left/ progressive perspective, is that she often touts the value of free markets, thus seeming to be oriented toward a market-based approach to solving the country's economic problems. That could easily lead to "trickle-down economics" that have been great for corporations and terrible for working people. However, many of her past positions and efforts have been devoted to raising the standard of living.

Clinton has stated that she won't raise taxes on the middle class, but she defines the middle class as those who make $250,000 or less a year, which presents quite a skewed sense of class composition in the United States. For example, the Pew Research Center defines the middle class as ending at a household income of $140,900.[154] Hillary's view might, again, be heavily influenced by the circles she runs in, but those circles are out of touch with the economic life of the country.

She's had a feminist view of Social Security for decades, stating in *Living History* that "the structure and notion of Social Security is based on the outdated notion of women as secondary breadwinners, or not as breadwinners at all."[155] She chaired a panel on Social Security in 1998 to look into the sexist assumptions embedded in its payment arrangements, which calculate benefits based on individual income and time in the workforce, therefore guaranteeing that most women will have lower benefits checks than men.

You could dig into Clinton's past and find both pro- and anti-worker moments. Her first work in Washington was on Senator Walter Mondale's subcommittee on migrant workers in 1971.[156] Yet she seemed to have crossed a picket line on her first date with Bill Clinton in New Haven; he charmed his way into a gallery during a widespread strike on campus by offering to pick up trash, and she followed. It's probably not fair, however, to put Bill Clinton's charm and willingness to impress a date onto the list of Hillary's anti-labor actions.[157] She didn't make a comment during her six years on the Walmart board in support of labor unions.[158] While in her tenure as Senator, she was a consistent ally of community groups such as ACORN, according to founder Wade Rathke, and "advocated for the group's housing programs and defended the Community Reinvestment Act, a 1977 law encouraging banks to make loans to people in low-income neighborhoods."[159] She has been a long-term and vocal advocate for equal pay for women in the workplace, as I mentioned above.[160]

She has consistently stressed a two-part requirement for her economic policies: if we cut welfare, we have to offer jobs. I think this repeated position about the need for employment is a useful hook for activists to use in holding Clinton accountable for the economic effects of any decisions she might make. In 2008, she ran to the left of President Obama on many economic issues, including a cabinet position "solely and fully devoted to ending poverty as we know it, that will focus the attention of our nation on this issue and never let it go."[161]

On the off-shoring of jobs, she states, "I know we can bring jobs and create jobs right here. I believe if we change the incentives in our tax code to recruit jobs here and we penalize those companies that are shipping jobs out, especially if they have received government money from you and me."[162] Clinton's website lists under the "Economy" tab a "plan to raise American incomes" that includes "creating good-paying jobs": "Hillary believes the defining economic challenge of our time is raising incomes for hardworking Americans." These jobs will be created by investing in infrastructure, environmentally-friendly jobs, and other projects such as tax breaks for companies that engage in profit-sharing with their employees.[163] Although efforts like profit-sharing will add a bump to a few lucky employees' paychecks, they don't offer structural change. I think all of these proposals are fine, but I wonder how much of a major role the president of the U.S. will actually have in reshaping the orientation of the economy with regard to working people.

One of the troubling elements of Clinton's position is with regard to free-trade agreements. Labor unions often find these agreements – like the North American Free Trade Agreement and the Trans-Pacific Partnership – undercut their bargaining power and result in a net loss of jobs. She did vote against the Central American Free Trade Agreement, which Bill Clinton publicly supported.[164]

She hardly mentions NAFTA in *Living History* and doesn't sing its praises even when she could have, but in her role as Secretary of State, she often touts the value of open international trade, as she does in *Hard Choices.* A large question remains over her role in the Trans-Pacific Partnership. She clearly told labor unions in 2015 that she did not work on the TPP during her time as Secretary of State. She:

subtly distanced herself from the trade policies associated with the 1990s....

Her spokesman, Nick Merrill, said Mrs. Clinton believed that any trade deal should protect American workers, raise wages and create jobs in the United States. 'The goal is greater prosperity and security for American families, not trade for trade's sake,' Mr. Merrill said in a statement.[165]

Yet there is clear evidence from direct Obama-administration aides and communications that she *did* support and help negotiate elements of the TPP.[166] The Panama Free Trade Agreement was another trade deal opposed by union activists and watchdog groups and supported by Clinton under the auspices of Obama.[167] Finally, Hillary Clinton had opposed a free trade agreement with Colombia during her presidential run in 2008, but then supported it in 2011; *International Business Times* notes this position change came about after a donation from a Canadian company with financial interests in Colombia.[168] Union representatives from Colombia contacted her with concerns about specific labor issues and instances of violence toward union organizers, and she did not respond.[169]

I don't know the extent to which Hillary had a choice in carrying out the Obama administration directives on this issue, but she could have been honest about these facts. To me, this issue – the unwillingness to be honest with labor unions – is more concerning than the somewhat circumstantial evidence about payouts from Wall Street. If Hillary regrets her involvement in anti-worker issues, that's fine, but she needs to definitely uphold her stated commitments to only signing trade agreements that preserve domestic jobs and the rights of workers here and abroad to protest bad working conditions.

CHAPTER 11
WHAT KIND OF PRESIDENT
WOULD HILLARY BE?

On the level of domestic politics, one of the main arguments in favor of Hillary Clinton offered by her supporters is that she knows how to get things done in the ramshackle and often horribly contentious constellation of Congressional politics. She has a proven ability to negotiate, to compromise, and to pass legislation. Others supporting Clinton claim with a good degree of accuracy that since they've liked Obama as President for two terms and that he cannot run anymore, Clinton is the logical extension of him and the next best thing. If one likes Obama's policy actions – which increasingly tacked toward the Bill Clinton "New Democrat" model over the eight years of his presidency – then Hillary Clinton is indeed the logical choice. The strong personal relationship forged between Obama and Clinton during her time as Secretary of State, and her clear deference to his authority, shows her to be a team player who is in effect anointed as the next Democratic Party favorite.

During the 2016 Democratic primary, Hillary Clinton and Bernie Sanders each tried to prove they would be engaged in more productive legislative work and would stick to principles. Emily Cadei writes in *Newsweek* that while Sanders was often viewed as more idealistic, Clinton and Sanders "ultimately took the same approach" of "working within the system to shape the congressional sausage-making....In other words, when it comes to big policy changes, neither is nearly as reckless or naïve as their critics would have you believe."[170]

Some believe that the ability to forge bipartisan coalitions is a necessary qualification for a U.S. president, as it is challenging to pass legislation when a Congress is deeply divided politically or polarized along party lines. Others believe the most vital function of the presidency is a rhetorical one in which national mission and identity are shaped; for someone with these criteria, Hillary Clinton's long connection to Washington, D.C., itself makes her suspect, as these relationships and alliances might shape her decisions more than her firm allegiance to a political stance.

Jamelle Bouie writes in *The Nation*:
Hillary Clinton is a triangulating corporate Democrat who forged her political identity

against a relentless, ideologically driven GOP and built her core support among the wealthy elites of the Democratic Party. The former makes her suspicious of (if not hostile to) the left on foreign and domestic policy, while the latter – coupled with her time as New York senator – makes her receptive to the failed ideas and expertise of Wall Street.[171]

For that reason, says Bouie, "the task for liberals – and the left more broadly – is to correct that blind spot in the party and, in the process, force Clinton to see that the 1990s are over, and the public is more than primed for a big swing."[172] Joan Walsh writes with more optimism, also in *The Nation,* "I believe she's evolved back to be the progressive Democrat she used to be, more progressive than her liberal husband."[173] Michelle Goldberg writes in *The Nation* that Clinton's "overall voting record in the Senate was to the left of both Obama and Joe Biden"[174] as well as John Kerry, an important element that has often been obscured during the Democratic primary in 2016 when candidates waged a massive display to differentiate themselves from each other. Either way, Clinton will look to the public for support for her agendas and will need insistent citizen input to pull her away from the philanthrocapitalism that has ensnared her husband.

At the level of temperament, I find myself surprised by how much I am drawn to Hillary as a leader: she's not a show-boat who plays politics for the sake of racking up points. She seems much less interested in exacting revenge than her husband was. She works hard, she's intelligent, pragmatic, and experienced. She has been through decades of continuous public scrutiny and crushing personal humiliation, yet manages to get up and smile in a way that seems genuine. She writes about her spiritual centeredness and her Methodism. She has cranked out books, and yes, she earned millions from them, but after reading two tomes I am impressed at the level of depth and detail, the über-focus that she brought to recording her positions. At a personal level, delving into her substantial backstory has convinced me that she will be a competent leader who will not be embittered or stunned at any point by the horrible game of politics in Washington or on the international stage, and I think that is a necessary qualification for the position of president. While the real-life movie of *Mr. Sanders Goes to Washington* would have been fascinating to observe, it's clear that Hillary will deliver little comparable entertainment value. She doesn't go in for grandstanding. In fact, she's controlled because we've made her that way. We think we know what we get with Hillary because she has been tested on the national and international stage. At the same time, the presidency itself might allow her a new latitude to be open about the agendas she cares about. The big show for Hillary might be very different than we have imagined it to be.

CHAPTER 12
A TINY SLICE OF A FEW POSITIONS NOT MENTIONED SO FAR

It would be impossible to cover all of the various issues that Clinton has covered both in her campaign or in her public work to date, so in this chapter I'll address just a few flashpoints that have differentiated her – and dogged her – over the years and in the run-up to the election.

Education

Like many, I have noted with concern that both Hillary and Bill were in favor of educational reforms that included increased standardized testing. Hillary's website lists her as "a key member shaping the No Child Left Behind Act, with the hopes that it would bring needed resources and real accountability to improve educational opportunities for our most disadvantaged students."[175] Instead of accountability and action, what the legislation has largely brought to the U.S. is a student population mired in standardized tests, which are then used to designate "failing schools." The failing schools – almost always in low-income areas where tax revenue is scarce and children deal with the weight of challenging home lives and parents struggling with the effects of poverty – are then punished with a variety of measures including state takeover, drastic leadership transitions, and corporate-driven initiatives that further undercut teachers' power in the districts. I would hope Hillary would move beyond testing as a strategy for improving education. She is now endorsed by two of the largest teachers' unions, whereas many backers of education "reform" including the Gates Foundation and the Walton Family Foundation (the family that owns Walmart), often have an implicit agenda that includes destruction of these unions as a method of "improving" education.[176]

Liza Featherstone writes in *The Nation* that Clinton "led the efforts by her husband's administration to weaken teachers' unions and scapegoat teachers – most of them women, large numbers of them black – for problems in the education system, implementing performance measures and firings that set a punitive tone for education reform nationwide."[177]

Although in the past she's supported charter schools, Hillary seems to be wavering on that front: "One reason I support improving our public school system through higher standards and greater accountability and oppose weakening it through vouchers is that it brings together children of all races, religions and backgrounds, and has shaped and sustained our pluralistic democracy."[178]

Her knowledge of early childhood education, and her strong support for it, is one of the bedrocks of her political career. She convened two White House conferences, one on Early Childhood Development and one on Childcare, while Bill was president, and his administration put forward $20 billion investment in childcare.[179]

Continued Global Survival
(The Environment)

Naomi Klein writes in *The Nation* that the need for firm and immediate action against climate change is one of the biggest reasons not to elect Hillary Clinton. Klein writes that it will be necessary "to go head-to-head with the two most powerful industries on the planet – fossil-fuel companies and the banks that finance them."[180] It's often been cited that Hillary's political allegiances are cemented with contributions from the fossil fuel industry, including a Super-PAC that donated $3.25 million as of March 2016.[181]

She voted against President George W. Bush's energy bill, which included $14.5 in energy industry tax breaks.[182] In *Hard Choices,* Hillary mentions that President Obama initially was not going to attend the 2009 Copenhagen climate talks, and that her insistence led him to attend. They together horned in on conversations that, while not binding, expressed the U.S.'s commitment to opening the conversation. On the other hand, her commitment to economic growth as a way to democratize societies leads her to endorse exploration of new energy markets as a way to stabilize economies and democracies, which might very well lead her to see expansion of energy markets as a key to political stability. She has come under fire for supporting fracking in countries across the globe as a way to develop energy self-sufficiency as a key to political stability.[183]

Bill McKibben, founder of the climate action group 350.org, takes Clinton to task for her ties to the fossil fuel industry, says she could have done more at the Copenhagen climate talks, and that she bungled an opportunity to show leadership on the issue of the Keystone XL Pipeline, a proposed expansion of an oil pipeline that runs from Canada to refineries in the U.S.; opponents say it only furthers dependence on fossil fuels. She expressed her concerns about the pipeline and came out against it in September 2015 after two years of not issuing a comment on the controversy.[184] Clinton has also come under fire for her acceptance of funding from corporations that conduct fracking, an energy extraction process that has been linked to a host of environmental messes from methane leaks to groundwater contamination and more. Here's the thing: fracking is basically another word for extraction of natural gas, and the HillaryClinton.com website is still chock-full of arguments in favor of domestically produced natural gas (which would, apparently, be fracking) as a key to energy self-sufficiency.[185] During her tenure as Secretary of State she seemed to support fracking, and she has said in the past that she supports fracking with regulations.[186] During her presidential campaign, she has seemed to move away from support for fracking in the face of environmental activists' resistance to the practice.[187] We live in a petroleum-based economy, and transitioning rapidly to something else is going to be rife with conflicts; however it's not always clear whether the environmental impacts of these choices are Hillary's first priority.

She does believe that global warming exists. She also says that climate change aggravates and contributes to global political instability including the refugee crisis in Syria.[188] So she has all the evidence to know that climate change exacerbates global instability, and she has set benchmarks in her campaign platform for transition to non-petroleum energy sources, but I'm not sure it's likely that confronting the petrochemical agenda will be front and center for her – though it needs to be for our survival.

Immigration

Hillary Clinton has taken a leftward swing on immigration, facing criticism for her past support for a "fence" between Mexico and the U.S. and her vague opposition to providing drivers' licenses to undocumented New Yorkers.[189] At a campaign stop in March 2016, Clinton said, "I will not deport children. I do not want to deport family members, either.... Stop the raids. Stop the roundups."[190] In this stance, she distanced herself from the Obama administration's immigration actions that have led to deportations.[191] Her positions outline detailed descriptions on paths to citizenship, including those for parents whose children are citizens, and for providing healthcare to all families regardless of citizenship status.[192]

Her current positions, in effect, would roll back pernicious elements of Bill Clinton's 1996 welfare reform, which restricted federal welfare benefits for those without social security numbers.[193] That measure has long been controversial because it denied federal benefits to those who, through their paycheck deductions, had nonetheless been paying into the system through wage deductions.

Reproductive Rights

Planned Parenthood and NARAL Pro-Choice America, two organizations that support women's access to abortion as well as other reproductive and women's healthcare causes, both endorsed Clinton; reproductive healthcare and abortion access are legal in the U.S., but are continually under fire from religious groups and state efforts to limit them. These efforts include 288 different state laws, violence, and anti-choice picketing at abortion clinics.[194] In the wake of the endorsements for Clinton, Bernie Sanders dismissed those non-profits as "the Establishment" presumably because of their longevity and their political profile.[195] But as Joan Walsh writes in *The Nation:*

I think it's hard to be truly establishment when dangerous men are shooting up your clinics, and the Republican Congress is persistently voting to strip you of your funding.... But I'm old enough to remember when feminists were told that our issues – 'cultural' issues like abortion and contraception – were costing Democrats elections, so couldn't we pipe down for a little while?[196]

Clinton's pro-choice stance includes her support for repeal of the Hyde Amendment, a law that makes it very difficult for low income women to obtain an abortion by prohibiting any federal funding, including Medicaid coverage, from going toward abortion costs.[197] Activists credit regular pressure on Clinton as being the reason she has steadily moved from her mid-1990s stance on abortion as a hopefully "rare" event to her current stance.

NARAL Pro-Choice American explains in its endorsement of Clinton: "Women expect to be in the workplace for our entire reproductive lives – both when we are not ready to parent and when we are growing our families. That makes being able to decide if and when to expand our families a foundational economic issue."[198] And, she's tough enough that she fought, in a good-natured way, with Mother Teresa over the right to abortion access.

LGBTQ Rights

Hillary Clinton has taken a long and cautious road on LGBTQ rights. She opposed gay marriage in her 2008 campaign,[199] and in the 1990s she supported the "Defense of Marriage" legislation signed by Bill Clinton.[200] This, however, was part of an evolution of positions that Bernie Sanders and President Obama also experienced, and the change happened because of activist public pressure on all candidates and office-holders.[201] Sanders, as one example, opposed gay marriage for his home state of Vermont in 2006 and avoided opposing the Defense of Marriage Act on moral grounds, instead claiming that it impinged on states' rights.[202]

In the lead-up to the Supreme Court Decision on Same-Sex Marriage in 2015, Hillary taped a video for the Human Rights Campaign in which she stated that she supported gay marriage, and she respected the views of those who didn't. As reported in the book *HRC:*

For years, friends of Hillary's had seen her struggle with the question of whether legalizing gay marriage could infringe on the rights or beliefs of religious groups, and she told her aides that she wanted to be respectful of their views even as her public position shifted….[a source involved in the discussion said,] 'she was pretty clear. But she was equally clear that she was not going to demonize people who disagreed with her on this.'

This seems to have been code for a delicate dance that played out over the late 1990s and early 2000s, as the country experienced a rapid swing in public opinion in favor of marriage equality that found many politicians following rather than leading on this issue. In some ways this is a continuation of the "Don't Ask, Don't Tell" logic employed during Bill Clinton's presidency. As often happens, a changing public forced its leaders to adapt their positions and stances.

While serving as Secretary of State, Hillary was a strong international advocate for gay rights, according to a colleague:

she had rewritten the department's rules so that same-sex partners of diplomats posted overseas would get the same benefits as husbands and wives; incorporated the protection and advancement of gay rights abroad as part of the core mission of American diplomats; and given a December 2011 speech to the UN Human Rights Council in which she compared the minority status of gays and lesbians to that of racial, religious, and ethnic minorities. The message to American diplomats, according to one source was, 'you can't fuck this up, because I'm going to hold you accountable,' and that's pretty stratospheric.[203]

In March 2016, she said on MSNBC that Nancy Reagan was an advocate of AIDS research, which enraged many in the gay community who lived through an era in which President Ronald Reagan and his wife were widely seen to have neglected the issue of AIDS when it exploded in the 1980s.[204]

Gun Control

In U.S. politics, the gun lobby and the right to bear arms is a flashpoint, given the number of massacres and the flailing about for causes and solutions. In the 2016 campaign, Clinton has distinguished herself by openly opposing the National Rifle Association, the powerful lobbying group that supports gun ownership. Hillary has advocated for stricter background checks, which are sometimes required when one purchases a gun or applies for a license to carry a firearm.[205] Gun massacres in the United States repeat themselves with reliability, and the issue has remained in the public eye especially after the mass shooting in a school in Newtown, Connecticut in 2012. In a general election, this might very well be a tough issue to take on and a deciding issue for rural voters. In 2008, she described herself as a "pro-gun churchgoer" in attempt to portray Barack Obama as out of touch with rural voters.[206] Some whom I polled informally identify themselves as single-issue voters on gun control and back Hillary for her current positions.

CHAPTER 13
H IS FOR HAWK

Let me take a strange way into Hillary Clinton's record in international affairs. I'd like to start with a column by a man whose points I somewhat agree with, yet whose rhetoric makes my blood boil. Patrick L. Smith wrote a column in *Salon* in March 2016 in which he said several true things: Hillary Clinton has a penchant for international intervention, and that could be bad. It could be more of the same that Obama has carried out, including the continued U.S. military presence and escalation in Afghanistan, our involvement in Honduras, and the toppling of Libya's government.

The problem with so much of the criticism of Clinton's role as Secretary of State is that there's so little information and so much sexism, even from the left. Smith calls Hillary "Clinton II" and "Nero." The column is titled, "As reckless as George W. Bush: Hillary Clinton helped create disorder in Iraq, Libya, Syria – and, scarier, doesn't seem to understand how."[207] This rhetoric sets up two clear camps and no other options; all I have to do is question the way Smith has phrased this, and I *am* Clinton II, I *am* an imperialist just like her, a woman who does not even get the dignity of being a separate human being from her husband.

Smith's essay *isn't* actually a piece about Clinton's foreign affairs missteps. It's about what Hillary Clinton "doesn't seem to understand." Without dwelling on her actual foreign policy, Smith quickly turns to anyone who might be even considering voting for her:

> Those who might be inclined to vote for Clinton are the responsible parties now. They must bear down on themselves, so that we can rid the forward-thinking side of our political conversation of its many encrustations – its mythologies, conventions, orthodoxies and the stale assumptions that have been placed over many years in some zone wherein they are taken to lie beyond questioning.

Encrustations? Patrick L. Smith, I agree with some of your points, but your pompous posturing is exactly what will drive people to vote for this she-demon you loathe. Smith writes, "No one can seriously question Hillary Clinton's influential role in creating the disorder that envelops us." So that's the current argument: after four years as Secretary of State, it's already Hillary's world and it's all already her fault. That is taking things a bit too far. Were any dudes in the house to make this shitstorm? Maybe Ronald Reagan or George W. Bush's Vice President Dick Cheney? Nope. Just Hillary.

Smith cites an article by a socialist feminist he agrees with. Then he cites another woman he disagrees with, calling her a "self-described" socialist feminist, as if her own self-description might be pending review. His argument veers to a larger critique of feminism in the US, which he sees as depoliticized and enthralled with American exceptionalism. Feminists who support Hillary, Smith claims, are doing it wrong: "Feminism must be recognized and deployed as a subset of humanism. Any other understanding of it renders it impotent in the advance of its own cause." In other words, the priorities of feminism are not up for debate; there are two positions, and if you support Hillary, you're not a humanist.

Guys, here's what you don't understand. That's exactly the kind of talk that makes a woman who has been stepped on her whole life just *want* a woman to claim power. Smith's column is a no-fly zone of male micro-aggression, a drone attack of well-intentioned mansplaining exceptionalism that turns to sexism instead of political positions. And that makes me want to vote for Hillary, just to piss him off.

A Tumblr page called "Texts from Hillary," created by Stacy Lambe in April 2012, used a photo of Clinton wearing sunglasses to imagine her texting world leaders. "Hey Hil, Watchu doing?" Obama supposedly texted her. Her imaged text back: "Running the world."[208] The image and similar that followed went viral for a few weeks, projecting a powerful, funny, and self-aware Clinton that captured favorable attention for her as Secretary of State. This is why she is beloved, because for a short moment it was okay for a woman to be in charge without having to be blamed for the entire course of Western Civilization.

Now back to serious amalgamation of facts, including reasoned critique of Hillary Clinton's role in U.S. empire-building and empire-sweeping-up. Clinton began her tenure as Secretary of State touting a concept of "smart power," which she described as a mixture of military might and diplomacy. Hillary Clinton is characterized as a "hawk" on international issues, meaning that she has a propensity for intervention and a general bias toward action.[209] Analysts point to two episodes from Bill Clinton's presidency as convincing her of the need for international intervention: "the American failure to prevent the Rwandan genocide in 1994, and the success, albeit belated, in bringing together an international military coalition to prevent greater bloodshed after 8,000 Muslims were massacred in Srebrenica during the Bosnian war."[210]

She supported American intervention in Libya, the troop surge in Afghanistan, and had recommended more direct involvement in Syria.[211] In each of these cases, you could argue that she was swayed by the potential loss of life had the U.S. not gotten involved, but many critics have argued that, with regard to Libya in particular, she underestimated the danger involved in deposing a dictator in a nation and leaving a power vacuum.

In general, Clinton views the U.S. as an "indispensable nation" with regard to the world stage, which some critics see as necessarily leading us into involvement around the globe. Anatoly Lieven writes in *The Nation* that "nationalist myths" blind Clinton and others to the idea that the American model might not be a sustainable or "universal path for the progress of mankind." Lieven argues that the U.S. will need to abandon the narrative of U.S. global primacy in favor of new cooperative models that privilege international goals, especially as we confront the destabilizing power of climate change. To address this global issue that could easily affect our allies,

Clinton will need to directly confront corporate and financial leaders both in the U.S. and abroad.[212]

Her time as Secretary of State has given her both a great deal of experience to draw on as well as her share of difficulties. She was working for President Obama during a time of great upheaval in the Middle East, so it's impossible to say that she got her way and pushed Obama around to military intervention against his will. At the same time, there's enough record of their disagreements to provide evidence that she was often willing to be more aggressive than other members of the administration.

This might seem obvious, but Hillary Clinton took her job as the Secretary of State seriously. Specifically, she seemed devoted to the idea of extending diplomatic relations to even nations with which the U.S. had has fraught relationships as a way to avoid military conflict or reorient relationships between nations. Her approach to diplomacy involved regular contact and personal relationships, using familiarity as a foundation for dialogue. In many ways this prioritization on regular contact seems preferable to posturing and rigid positions likely to escalate conflict. Personal ties did not prevent several controversies during her time as Secretary of State, though Clinton might argue that to expect anything less would be hopelessly naive.

First, some non-terrible stuff: Clinton began her tenure as Secretary of State by advocating a "pivot" toward Asia that included greater engagement in the region but also possible containment of China, which one analyst believed could back the U.S. into a major conflict in the future.[213] Throughout her four years as Secretary of State, Hillary opened a relationship with Burma and restored diplomatic ties, which led eventually to U.S. support for new democratic elections. Imprisoned leader Aung San Suu Kyi, a longtime advocate for democratic reforms, was released from house arrest and traveled to Washington D.C. to tell American leaders, "The sanctions worked."[214] She included the rights of women and girls in many negotiations internationally, and she pushed for attention to innovating projects such as the use of less toxic cook stoves for women in rural areas of the globe. That fact didn't make headlines, but it's important.

Now for some difficult stuff.

Honduras

About five months after Clinton took office in January 2009, a coup erupted in Honduras. The elected president, Manuel Zelaya, was forced into exile; the U.S. officially opposed the coup, but wasn't willing to stick its neck out for Zelaya because he had become linked to left-wing governments in the region (which would be within his rights as president of a nation). After the coup, the State Department urged Hillary to shift the negotiations from the Organization of American States to private mediation that would be less favorable to Zelaya. Other sources inside the State Department were pushing her to declare the region under a military coup, which would have stopped non-humanitarian sanctions and in effect would have said that Zelaya was robbed of his rightful post. Hillary declined to do so; new elections took place, but the military coup-backed government remained in place.[215] As a result, Honduras has descended into violence, spurred by an increase in drug-related crime and corruption on the part of police and the military, with anti-government protestors and peasant organizers particularly at risk.[216]

Haiti

The Clintons have a long history of involvement in Haiti. Bill Clinton sent 20,000 U.S. troops to the country in 1994 to return democratically elected leader Jean-Bertrand Aristide to power after a military coup. Bill Clinton was later named a UN special envoy to the country, and after the 2010 earthquake the Clintons were actively involved in raising millions for relief efforts. In 2012, they supported financing for an industrial park. Critics in Haiti reported that the aid money has not been spent fully and that promised jobs from the industrial park did not materialize. In 2011, Hillary pressured the country to include a popular singer, Michel Martelly, on the ballot for the country's presidential elections, after another candidate was feared to be involved with voting fraud.[217] Martelly, who won the election, was widely seen as autocratic and inept, then left power without naming a successor in 2016. [218]

Afghanistan and Pakistan

Possibly because of her long-term exposure to politics, Hillary Clinton feels a strong responsibility to address issues caused by previous U.S. interventions. It is important for her to not abandon Afghanistan, as she believes the U.S. did in 1989 when the Soviet troops withdrew, and which she sees as creating the current instability in the region.[219] Disagreeing with the positions of Vice President Joe Biden and President Obama, she backed a surge of troops into Afghanistan in 2014.[220] She said she would evaluate the continued presence of troops in Afghanistan if elected.[221]

During her time as Secretary of State, her relationship with Pakistan was in some ways a model of her combined active intervention and diplomacy. She supported the assassination of Osama Bin Laden in Pakistan without the country's permission, but she advocated for apologizing for the accidental death of two dozen soldiers in November 2011 during a NATO airstrike:

> Hillary believed that 'the ability to admit you're wrong is a sign of strength, not weakness,' one of her senior aides said later. Hillary's elevation of Pakistan, through her visits and direct engagement with both the country's leaders and its people, had helped make her the American official with the most credibility in the country. 'I'm still shocked that the Pakistanis love her and hate Obama for the same damn policy,' said one senior administration official focused on Pakistan. 'That is a successful operation.'[222]

In *Hard Choices,* Clinton recounts visits to town hall meetings in Pakistan where she knew she was going to be given a hard time, but didn't mind, as she was committed to developing a personal familiarity with people in the country. At one of these meetings, a young woman questioned her sharply on use of drones: "...looking at her, I thought back to my own days as a student who was quick to question authority figures. Young people often fearlessly say what the rest of us are thinking but are too cautious to speak out loud. If I had been born in Pakistan, who knows, perhaps I would be standing where she was now."[223]

Palestine, Israel, Iran and International Arms Deals

Hillary Clinton was a key player toward the very end of her tenure as Secretary of State in negotiating a cease-fire between Israel and Palestine. In return for a Palestinian ceasefire, Israel opened crossings on the Gaza border, bringing Mohamed Morsi, then president of Egypt, into the agreement.[224] However, when she addressed the American Israel Public Affairs Committee, she pledged to bring Israel's right-wing Prime Minister Benjamin Netanyahu to the White House; Netanyahu has pledged to oppose any two-state solution to the Israel/Palestine conflict.[225] Howard Dean describes her as "the principal author of the sanction on Iran that brought them to the table,"[226] and she apparently did so even against the wishes of one of her billionaire supporters, pro-Israel Haim Saban.[227]

People seem glad to see that she can stand up to donors, because critics have also raised questions about the extent to which contributors to the Clinton Foundation – including defense companies and foreign governments – were rewarded with international arms deals. David Sirota and Andrew Webb of *International Business Times* reported in May 2015: "Under Clinton's leadership, the State Department approved $165 billion worth of commercial arms sales to 20 nations whose governments have given money to the Clinton Foundation, according to an *International Business Times* analysis of State Department and foundation data. That figure… represented nearly double the value of American arms sales made to the those countries and approved by the State Department during the same period of President George W. Bush's second term."[228]

The Clinton Foundation agreed to disclose any donations from foreign governments just before Hillary Clinton took over as Secretary of State, but "officials at the State Department and White House raised no issues about potential conflicts related to arms sales." However,

> 'The word was out to these groups that one of the best ways to gain access and influence with the Clintons was to give to this foundation,' said Meredith McGehee, policy director at the Campaign Legal Center, an advocacy group that seeks to tighten campaign finance disclosure rules. 'This shows why having public officials, or even spouses of public officials, connected with these nonprofits is problematic.'

As with Clinton's domestic financial ties, nobody doing any digging has found a cause-and-effect relationship or a "smoking gun," but there's a lot of money, influence, and power swirling.

CHAPTER 14
FOREIGN POLICY NIGHTMARES
AND QUAGMIRES

When Hillary Clinton was Secretary of State, the issue of her propensity for intervention came to the fore, touching off Americans' deep fear of becoming embroiled in another Vietnam, as we are currently somewhat engaged in Iraq and Afghanistan. Many in the U.S. who are Baby Boomers and younger feel that wherever the U.S. lands on the globe, we can't help but make everything worse and leave civil war in our wake. Despite coming of age in the 1960s, Hillary will have none of this hesitancy; she seems to have hope that she can make the world a better place with U.S. involvement. She did say in February 2016 that sending troops to Syria and Iraq would be a terrible mistake; I desperately hope she continues to hold that assessment. [229] What she might be underestimating – or be out of touch with – is the deep fatigue and the costs of military involvement here at home, and the degree to which years and years of repeated tours of duty have shattered families and lives both at home and abroad.

Iraq

Hillary Clinton's 2002 vote for the Iraq War has come to play a central role in the 2016 Democratic primary. I would argue this is not actually the most telling piece of information about her foreign policy, partly because many other people who have at times been considered Democratic presidential contenders – Joe Biden and John Kerry – also voted for the war in the heated insanity of the false threat of "Weapons of Mass Destruction."[230] The *Rolling Stone* editorial endorsement of her says, the decision was "a huge error, one that many made, but not one that constitutes a disqualification on some ideological purity test."[231] Yet it must be considered.

Clinton says, "I came to deeply regret giving President Bush the benefit of the doubt on that vote. He later assured that the resolution gave him the sole authority to decide when the clock had run out on weapons inspections...with UN weapons inspectors pleading for just a few more weeks to finish the job."[232] Colin Powell's State Department had been "all but shut out of postwar planning," which shaped her own agenda for her tenure as Secretary of State. She adds, "I should have stated my regret sooner and in the plainest, most direct language possible. I'd gone most of the way there...

but I held out against using the word *mistake.* I still got it wrong. Plain and simple."[233] She piled onto this mistake by claiming initially that she supported the war in part because President George W. Bush promised her $20 million[234] in aid for New York after the 9/11 attack.

Libya

After protests sparked through the Middle East in Arab Spring of 2011, Muammar Qaddafi of Libya was rumored to be moving toward a massacre of rebels in the area of Benghazi as violence escalated. President Obama and others initially resisted involvement. British Prime Minister David Cameron and the French Prime Minister expressed enthusiasm for Libyan intervention.[235] Clinton "had a new opportunity to support the historic change that had just swept out the leaders of its neighbors Egypt and Tunisia. And Libya seemed a tantalizingly easy case – with just six million people, no sectarian divide and plenty of oil."[236]

In discussions over whether to intervene as part of a NATO effort, Clinton spoke of her connection to the Libyan opposition leader, and many point to her involvement as swaying the debate and switching the U.S. to advocate for not only a no-fly zone but more direct intervention.

France then announced that its planes were already in the air, which in effect forced the U.S.'s hand toward approving military action. Gradually, the mission expanded from preventing Qaddafi's initial attacks to protecting citizens more broadly.

In the ensuing months, Hillary maintained an interest in keeping diplomatic personnel on the ground. Some would say this was because she was protecting a legacy of her own. Ambassador J. Christopher Stevens, one of the four Americans killed in the attack on the U.S. diplomatic compound in Benghanzi on Sept. 11, 2012, had asked the State Department to maintain the same level of security support at multiple points, but was denied his request. After the first and second attacks in Benghanzi, all hell broke loose for Clinton: Republicans were keen to know how responsible she was and whether tighter security could have prevented the attack. The Republican obsession with who knew what and when failed to turn up enough material for a scandal.

Jason Chaffetz, U.S. Representative from Utah, critiqued the setup in Libya as being too loose and oriented to diplomacy without enough military protection. He opposed the decision to go to war in Libya and "blamed Stevens's death on Hillary's desire to see the intervention prove wise.... 'I just think her push for normalization [of diplomatic relations] at the sacrifice of security cost people their lives and that was a cultural push from this administration, and I think from her, personally.'"[237]

The larger issues are: first, what to do with a state in chaos when we, in effect, created the vacuum, and second, whether Hillary Clinton's political defense of her own choices will allow for reflection and correction when it comes to larger policy orientation toward intervention.

In Fall 2015, she said at a hearing on Benghazi, "We have learned the hard way when America is absent, especially from unstable places, there are consequences....Extremism takes root, aggressors seek to fill the vacuum, and security everywhere is threatened, including here at home."[238] The question, then, is whether she thinks we can be everywhere, and what that will cost. The bad news is that instability in Libya has contributed to instability in the region and given ISIS a base, and weapons from Qaddafi's arsenals have made their way to Syria.[239]

Syria
Syria also erupted with hopeful demonstrations during the Arab Spring in 2011

that have since devolved into civil war against a repressive regime, and Syria's president Bashir al-Assad is being supported by Russia's Vladimir Putin. In her book *Hard Choices* Hillary calls Syria a "wicked" problem in the Boston sense of the word: "wicked complicated." Hillary has made some wacky, scary policy pronouncements, including calling for a "no-fly zone" in Syria, which would make Russia very upset. *Al Jazeera* describes the request for a no-fly zone as calling for a regime change without actually using those words[240]. Just so we all understand, calling for another country's government to go away, even if you don't like that government, is *hawkish*. Clinton advocated for more arms to support Syrian rebels and Obama demurred.

Hillary's attention to Syria goes back at least to 2003, when she co-sponsored the "Syrian Accountability Act" of 2003, which imposed sanctions despite the gradual liberalization of the Assad regime as a way to urge the country to not support terrorism.

Jeffrey Sachs calls Syria "the crowning disaster" of Hillary Clinton's time as Secretary of State and says she was too accepting of the CIA assessment that removal of Bashir al-Assad in August 2011 would be straightforward and rapid,[241] but I'm not sure what she could have done to oppose CIA assessments or covert operations. Even though she is, by some accounts, already running the world, she was not President in 2011. If she becomes President, however, we will need her to show caution in engaging with other nations and their troubled regimes, even if she feels we have a duty to intervene to right a historical wrong or to bring the model of America anywhere else in the world.

What is deeply worrisome is that Hillary Clinton said in late 2015 that she thinks Syria should be approached with "more airstrikes and an expanded deployment of special operations troops to assist local ground forces" to not only contain ISIS but to eradicate it.[242] Clinton supports more direct arming of rebels as well as continued use of drone strikes. Some of Clinton's statements in December 2015 seemed to indicate that regime change in Syria was a necessary precondition to fighting ISIS.[243] So in other words: we might get involved militarily, on the ground, in Syria, or wherever ISIS seems to be. I'm going to go out on a limb and say that's a bad idea. But I'm also going to say that I (unlike every other political commentator everywhere) have no idea how to defeat or defuse or placate ISIS. I'm glad it's not my job. Anyone who wants that job must be crazy, but I wish them luck, because they'll need it.

Thoughts on World Peace
Because I started with Patrick L. Smith, I'll end with another piece of commentary, this time from Ijeoma Oluo in *The Establishment,* in the brilliantly entitled piece "How to Not Be An Asshole This Election Season." Oluo, like me, "will never forgive Hillary for voting for the Iraq war. I don't think we should ever leave drone strikes out of Obama's biography." But, she says, it's time to stop pretending that the president is going to be a pure superhero:

> Last I checked, all our candidates are still running to be a part of our global system of shady, bloody, international shit. None of them, not even Bernie, will avoid drone strikes where suspected ISIS terrorists and more likely a few sleeping families reside. None of them will stop financing bloody dictators. Not one. There is no savior on the ballot, so stop accusing supporters of your opposing side of genocide, as if your candidate is going to bring about world peace.[244]

Ijeoma Oluo has a point: this is the presidency of the United States. If we want to change the United States, it's going to take more than picking one person to be amazing for four years so we can all relax, because that's not how real political change works. We citizens of the U.S. were born in an imperialist capitalist shit-storm. Even if the U.S. were to somehow become an amazing democratic socialist country, the road to get there would be messy. We will get more people to sign on to our vision of social change if we stop threatening to purge everyone for their lack of purity and instead focus on platforms and issues. Clinton is not your socialist feminist wonder woman. Are you surprised? You shouldn't be.

CHAPTER 15
CLOSING THOUGHTS ON
THE HOT BOX AND THE
BALLOT BOX

Kathleen Geier writers in *The Nation* that the
Left shouldn't fall for Hillary Clinton and "enable
neoliberalism." I agree. Some people in the country
who consider themselves "the Left" – a term that
is to the left of "progressive" – planned to support
Bernie Sanders even after his campaign, as he has
promised to transform his network into a social
movement. And that's great. Some think that any
tangling with the Democratic Party weakens social
movements, and others are trying to determine
if the Democrats can play a role in real progress.
The neoliberal Clintons were forged in reaction to
Reagan and later to Newt Gingrich. This doesn't
give the Clintons a pass, but it puts them – and
even their empire-building – in context. Not all
evils are the same; sometimes you *do* pick the
lesser evil, not because you love it, but because it's
slightly safer. And you do that with clear eyes, as
Hillary likes to say – though maybe at this point in
the game, we should look beyond this outmoded
position and triangulate somewhere toward hope.

Some people are very supportive of Hillary, for the reasons I've tried to explore in this volume. Others are so against her that they are driving their fellow progressives *toward* her. It's fascinating, as is the degree to which progressives savaged each other in Spring 2016 over the good fortune of having had two reasonable and competent candidates for President in the Democratic primaries. The *Rolling Stone* described the primary this way:

> The debates between Clinton and Sanders have been inspirational; to see such intelligence, dignity and substance is a tribute to both of them. The contrast to the banality and stupidity of the GOP candidates has been stunning. It's as if there are two separate universes, one where the Earth is flat and one where it is round; one where we are a country that is weak, flailing and failing; the other, an America that is still a land of hopes and dreams.[245]

Granted, that commentary was written in March. Even a month later the gloves had come off and Bernie had called Hillary unqualified for the role of President.

Hillary Clinton is a hawk; at first I thought this argument was just another way to distinguish her from Sanders in the Democratic primary, but I've become more convinced that is true. I even think that many potential Trump supporters were drawn to him because he's made noise about not getting involved in conflicts abroad. Clinton underestimates how many potential Trump supporters know or are veterans, how deeply fatigued and damaged the nation is by our military engagement around the world, and how other stances are vital.

I believe or hope that Hillary takes strong positions on the international stage out of a sense of responsibility for the troubles that others have started, as opposed to making up evidence for the sake of seeking revenge. But I think when you're embroiled in conflicts for a long time, as she has been, it may be difficult to shift views about other long-standing regimes or to operate with as much flexibility and openness as she claims she does.

I believe, based on what I have read, that Hillary's second major redeeming quality is not purity but that she responds to social movement pressure. The U.S. currently has a huge social movement pushing left. We are now, at least briefly, allowed to say the word "socialism" in public without getting fired or arrested (I'm exaggerating, but in a slightly uncomfortable and semi-serious way; in the U.S. Sanders has been so fascinating because very few people are open democratic socialists, as we are just *now* waking up from the Cold War). Okla Elliott writes in *Bernie Sanders: The Essential Guide* (also in the Squint series) that part of Sanders' contribution to the 2016 elections is that he forced Clinton "to adopt many of his policy positions."[246]

Some people like Hillary Clinton. Some feminists in particular are having their feminist politics sharpened in interesting ways as a result of interactions with other progressive/feminist/lefties. This doesn't mean the Hillary supporters are "dumb"; it means that the next iteration in this fascinating feminist dialectic is going to have great analysis about how to not alienate sections of a movement's potential constituency.

While I was writing this passage in the midst of the Democratic primary, I was toggling back and forth between the manuscript and Facebook for a break, as one does. A friend posted an article and tagged me. I wrote something like "Thanks!" Then beneath my comment appeared a long comment about Bernie Sanders from someone named Matt Saraceno who described Hillary as "a centrist with bad judgment. Nothing more. We expect the leader of the free world to have Bernie's judgment and character. There are no redeeming qualities Hillary possesses. Except we are told she has a vagina." Yikes! "Nothing more" and "no redeeming qualities." Was this convincing political argumentation or what? (Though my vagina does often give great policy advice.)

I checked out his profile and it was empty: no interests, no friends, no workplaces, and only posts about Bernie on his wall. A Bernie Bot. Or else Hillary has suddenly gotten so web-savvy that she's posing as Bernie Bots to drive people to her camp? The possibilities are endless.

Both the embrace of and the hatred for Hillary Clinton share one thing in common: the confused liberal hope that a president will magically make our problems go away. No, he or she will not. The president will always need progressive candidates in Congress, and those lower-visibility races are more difficult to mobilize around. The responsibility lies with us. Hillary Clinton has been described as a "boardroom liberal," and yet she is also a specific kind of boardroom liberal, different from her husband and more responsive to social movements. However, the social movements need to be there to push her. The people who claim they would have voted for Bernie but will not vote for Hillary betray a lack of real investment in political change, because the way you achieve change is through social movements, and a movement is much harder to organize than an election campaign.

As I was finishing this book, Bill Clinton made headlines again, this time for yelling back at Black Lives Matter protestors who were yelling at him about the legacy of mass incarceration that worsened after his crime bill. He handled it terribly – but again, this is not a book about Bill. Hillary's own moments have been different. She has had horrible moments of her own with regard to Black Lives Matter and with the African-American community. In June 2015, she visited a church near Ferguson, Missouri, where the unarmed teenager Michael Brown was shot to death by police, an event that helped spark the Black Lives Matter movement. Her visit occurred after the racially motivated shooting of nine people in an African-American church by a white supremacist in Charleston, South Carolina in 2015. At her visit she said, "All lives matter," which has become the clueless/aggressively hurtful response to Black Lives Matter activists and evidence of Black people's continual erasure.[247] But she was there at that church, trying in her own clumsy, pant-suited, earnest way.

Black Lives Matter activists interrupted one of her speeches in October 2015 about her criminal justice reform platform with shouts of "Black Lives Matter," and her response was, "Yes, yes they do," and then she kept on with the speech. Earlier in October, DeRay Mckesson, one of the Black Lives Matter movement leaders, sat down with Clinton to talk about her views on racial justice. He said to *Huffington Post*, "In the end, I felt heard...It was a tough conversation, and we didn't agree about every approach or everything. But she was willing to be pushed, and it was a candid conversation, and that's important."[248]

Hillary Clinton thinks activists are important, and her beliefs about activism are different from Bill's. Hillary Clinton has been engaging with social movements since she was an undergraduate at Wellesley reading Saul Alinksy. Michelle Goldberg writes in *The Nation*:

> Sixteen years ago, the late Barbara Olson, who served as chief investigative counsel to one of the House committees that investigated the Clintons in the 1990s, wrote *Hell to Pay: The Unfolding Story of Hillary Rodham Clinton*. In it, Olson warned: 'Hillary is a woman animated by a lifelong ambition. That ambition is to make the world accept

the ideas she embraced in the sanctuaries of liberation theology, radical feminism, and the hard left.' These were the words of a paranoid fanatic. Yet if, after all these years, Clinton were elected on a pro-childcare, pro-healthcare, pro-family-leave platform, it would represent a profound historical victory over the right-wing reaction that has dogged her for most of her life. Whether that's enough of a victory to excite today's ascendant left remains to be seen.[249]

In *Hard Choices,* Clinton described her agenda for travel as Secretary of State: "I made it clear that I wanted to get out beyond the Foreign Ministries and palaces and meet with citizens, especially community activists and volunteers; journalists; students and professors; business, labor, and religious leaders, the civil society that helps hold governments accountable and drives social change." In a 1998 speech she said, "I had compared a healthy society to a three-legged stool, supported by a responsible government, an open economy, and a vibrant civil society. That third leg of the stool was too often neglected."[250] If progressives in the U.S. are unhappy with Hillary's positions or her foreign policy in particular, we must respond to those choices in a way that does not degrade women and have the side-effect of driving women from politics.

Anna Galland, executive director of MoveOn.org Civic Action, was quoted in an article in *The Nation*: "The path to winning requires the Democratic presidential candidates to understand that the center of power in this country is no longer Third Way corporate 'centrism'....The political center of gravity is now a populist center of gravity, and everyone needs to reckon with that. I think her campaign is savvy, and they will."[251] The question, however, is what will happen to Hillary's populist positions after the campaign is over. If she becomes president, progressives have two choices: to hold her accountable or to devolve into misogyny and an attack on her entire past that many re-gressive elements of the electorate will welcome for all the wrong reasons.

Feminist scholar Johanna Brenner describes the dynamics within feminist movements over time:

> [T]he politics of middle-class feminists also shift depending on the levels of militancy, self-organization, and political strength of women in the working classes....While neoliberalism extinguished the radical promise of the second wave, it has also

created the material basis for the renewal
and spread of socialist feminist movements
led by working-class women – whether
employed in the formal economy, the
informal economy, in the country-side, or
doing unwaged labor.[252]

In other words, middle-class feminists can be
moved depending on the strength of working-
class women's organization. We can't imagine that
Hillary is going to embody our hopes and dreams
or that she will become a socialist. She's not. Only
organizing can push her toward specific public
demands.

Brenner points to cross-class organizing
like the National Welfare Rights Organization,
which she says broke down the divide between talk
of "needs" and "rights" in the 1970s:

Incorporating the ideas of working-class
women of color activists, socialist feminists
articulated a politics of reproductive
rights that reached beyond the language of
choice. Reproductive rights included the
right to be mothers and to raise children in
dignity and health, in safe neighborhoods,
with adequate income and shelter....
Some of these demands can be fought for
and won under capitalism – for example,

the outlawing of racist sterilization or
discrimination against lesbian mothers
– but wholesale adoption would be
incompatible with capitalism....[S]ocializing
the labor of care required confronting
capitalist class power. It was here that
twentieth century social-welfare feminism
foundered.[253]

In 2016 we saw a proto-social movement in the
U.S. filled with people excited by a Democratic
presidential candidate who basically said
capitalism sucks, look what it's doing to the world.
The question is how to turn that desire and position
into a real social movement. Candidates do not
make social change, nor do they make political
capital. They spend it. People and movements
make political capital with their actions and their
demands.

Richard Yeltsin writes in *The Nation:*
[T]he state of the left is that it has a
very strong intellectual/academic/media
infrastructure, but it needs many more
rank-and-file adherents and a movement
culture if it is to accomplish what the right
of Barry Goldwater/William F. Buckley/
Strom Thurmond/Newt Gingrich managed
– the seizing of a major party. For now,

Clinton is more likely than anybody else to be elected the next Democratic president. If this happens, it will be at once historic and banal.[254]

Only a social movement with positions beyond a bipartisan hatred can push Clinton to the right positions, but it's much harder to organize around a specific demand. Organizing around hating Hillary is easy, but it's not the same as organizing around political positions.

Ultimately, the tension of the 2016 primary season had to do with a large-scale push to find an "outside" candidate. More than half the U.S. wants off the ride, and many were drawn to Sanders or Trump for that reason. These days, American politics is best understood not in a Right vs. Left spectrum but as a quadrant, with top left and right being comfortable with insider politics, money in politics, corporate interests and lobbying. Clinton resides in the upper-left. The electorate, I would argue, is U-shaped, and a surprising number of working-class and middle-class men at the bottom of the U in particular see themselves as equally pulled to Trump or Bernie Sanders. This is an important phenomenon that has barely gotten coverage; I wrote about it with a generous view in *Salon.com* as connected to the notion of working-class male identity. In its grimmer visage, after reading one too many anti-Hillary commentary pieces, I am listening again to what some of those voters are saying, which is "Anyone but Hillary." The fact that that is a political position held on the left and the right – that Trump's hate-fueled hyper-capitalism and Bernie Sanders' democratic socialism seem equal – is frightening and points to, if nothing else, a missed opportunity to educate the American electorate about the nuances and benefits of democratic socialism. Many of these same people may have shrugged their shoulders or not known about Wall Street payouts to candidates in the long history of elections, but now they know, if nothing else, that Hillary somehow runs Wall Street. Does she? No, she does not. And if that's the takeaway from this primary season, it's a disservice to voters who need to know how American capitalism really works and how it is screwing them. They are not being screwed via a speaking fee from Goldman Sachs; the system is much bigger, more complex, and more entrenched than a single charge of collusion. Johanna Brenner writes, "Feminism and other movements against oppression must be cross-class movements." But "anybody but Hillary" isn't a movement. There are no politics there besides "not that... that... woman."

Hillary Clinton will in all likelihood act as a continuation of President Obama's presidency. I cried when President Obama was inaugurated because he was an African-American man with a background in organizing who promised change, and he would be our next president, and that was historic and wonderful. People like me (and most of us are guilty of sloppy thinking and political fatigue) supported Obama as the anointed one, and then had a tendency to look the other way at his foreign policy decisions and domestic errors as long as we possibly could. Some of the people who mostly gave Obama a pass and defended him against the Right now think that Hillary is the devil incarnate. And that is sheer hypocrisy.

This foray into Hillaryland has been very thought-provoking for me. While I was excited on an intellectual level by the Bernie Sanders campaign, and while I voted for Bernie Sanders in the Connecticut primary, I've also had moments of unease, as well as a reconsideration of my relationship to feminist movements. I've been involved in economic and racial justice activism for most of my adult life. I have relied upon feminist activists at every step of the way, from my job to my personal life to politics. As I think about the Hillary campaign, I think about how very much I have relied upon the gains of feminism, and the ways in which certain swathes of the left seem willing to take those gains for granted. I've needed a sexual assault hotline, an advocate for gender discrimination in the workplace, a feminist friend to help me get shit clear in my head, an affordable daycare, coaching on abuse in relationships and salary negotiations and harassment at work, a domestic violence center, a support group, a solidly feminist therapist, and a reproductive healthcare clinic. I have needed feminists to survive. Being a woman is hard in a way that a man will never understand, and feminist theory and feminists have helped me put my head and body back together over and over.

Now, some of those feminists who kept me alive are excited for Hillary; these feminists are being derided for wanting Hillary to be president *because* she's a woman. While that's not a revolutionary goal, it's a goal as important and moving to some people as having a Black man in the White House. And Hillary is not just *any* woman; she is a woman who has taken good positions as well as bad with regard to women's lives. Those positions are what her supporters are excited about.

I understand why some women want Hillary.

When your body has marked you as "outside" your entire life, when you have to constantly be on guard against sexism or racism or ableism, political awakening can come in the form of that visceral response in the hope that another outsider body will carry the understanding and make change. And that is feminism, too: the notion that we are embodied and that the experience of our bodies matters as women. So even if I am in favor of Bernie Sanders' economic policies and leery of Hillary's high-finance connections and tendency to act too quickly in the affairs of other nations, I'm not going to trash those feminists who support Hillary. In fact, the ugliness of the primary campaign has drawn me closer to anyone who's talking deep convincing feminism and away from anyone who's spouting easy dehumanization and misogyny. Calling someone "not a real feminist" is not the same thing as showing them important information about Hillary's involvement in the violence occurring in Honduras. Mocking someone for their desire to lead is not the same thing as a reasoned political argument. We are in a messy movement together. We can only bring each other along if we talk to each other. And we will need to in the coming months and years, in order to continue to hold Hillary accountable and if the range of demands brought forth by the Sanders campaign will ever have hope of being enacted.

I will be voting for Hillary in November. No one should confuse a vote for Clinton with support for every single one of her positions or actions; that's not what a presidential election has ever meant. The choices are too narrow. No matter what happens, our next job is to keep up the level of political engagement – with respect and dignity for all – that will help us develop a livable future.

HIDDEN TRACK:
THINGS HILLARY CLINTON LIKES

1. Headbands
2. The phrase "clear-eyed"
3. A zone of privacy
4. Action: she's impatient and likes to see results
5. Other people's creative ideas
6. Long meetings
7. Information
8. Brooches
9. Eleanor Roosevelt
10. Skiing
11. Jigsaw puzzles
12. Bill's hands (seriously, she goes on about them at length)
13. Oscar de la Renta
14. Joni Mitchell
15. Tabasco

Hillary Quotes:

"Bill often reminds me of the boy who is digging furiously in a barn filled with manure. When someone asks why, he says, 'With all this manure, there's got to be a pony in here somewhere.'"[255]

"When people ask me how I kept going during such a wrenching time, I tell them that there is nothing remarkable about getting up and going to work every day, even when there is a family crisis at home. Every one of us has had to do it at some time in our lives, and the skills required to cope are the same for a First Lady or a forklift operator. I just had to do it all in the public eye."[256]

ACKNOWLEDGMENTS

I'm letting down the women of the world, or I'm just being radically honest: research for this book involved developing a thumbnail history of a good chunk of U.S. domestic and international history. This was a challenge on a tight deadline, and as a result I may have misrepresented some of these points; my goal here was to bring threads together at a particular moment, not to offer in-depth histories of the conflicts that I have inevitably given short-shrift to. I'm grateful for the tight deadline and general scope of the series, which kept me from falling down the rabbit hole.

Thanks, first, to Kelly Davio and Todd Swift of Eyewear Publishing for giving me the chance to do this project, and to Okla Elliott for recommending me. Thanks to my household presidential historian Cliff Price and my number-one financial advisor and son, Ivan.

Writing and research and political friends who have supported me with the data and understanding in this project: Thanks to my writer support crew: Elizabeth Hilts, Sandy Rodriguez Barron, Nalini Jones, and Rachel Basch. For organizing support, political theory, and friendship:

Jocelyn Boryczka and the ladies of the Round Table: Emily, Anna, Kris, and Gwen. Thanks to Johanna Brenner, the folks at Solidarity for helping me hone my understanding of neoliberalism, and friends who shared their insights to help me come up with an outline for my research, including Anna March, Maria Marmanides, Nick Mancuso, Julie Farrar, Alice Sadaka, Anne Panning, Monica Kieser, MaryKatherine Ramsey, Beth Boquet, Marissa Landrigan, Mary Lide, Bernice Olivas, and Susan Smith Daniels, Colin Hosten, Elizabeth Lantz, Brian Clements, and William Anthony Connolly.

ENDNOTES

1 Jonathan Allen, Amie Parnes, *HRC: State Secrets and the Rebirth of Hillary Clinton*. Broadway Books, 2015. p. 249.

2 Ibid.

3 http://www.salon.com/2012/10/30/obama_last_of_the_new_democrats/

4 Daniel Gross, "How Hillary and Bill Clinton Parlayed Decades of Public Service into Vast Wealth," *Fortune*, Feb. 15, 2016.

5 Ibid.

6 Ibid.

7 Tom Gerencer, "Hillary Clinton Net Worth." *Money Nation*. April 2, 2016.

8 Robert D. McFadden, "Dorothy Rodham, Mother and Mentor of Hillary Clinton, is Dead at 92." *The New York Times*, Nov. 1, 2011.

9 http://www.ontheissues.org/celeb/Hillary_Clinton_Civil_Rights.htm

10 Mark Leibovich, "In Turmoil of '68, Clinton Found a New Voice." *The New York Times*, Sept. 5, 2007.

11 Ibid.

12 Alana Goodman, "The Hillary Letters: Hillary Clinton, Saul Alinsky Correspondence Revealed." *The Washington Free Beacon*, Sept. 21, 2014.

13 http://www.scribd.com/doc/240077031/The-Hillary-Letters

14 Mark Leibovich, "In Turmoil of '68, Clinton Found a New Voice." *The New York Times*, Sept. 5, 2007.

15 Frank Marafiote, "Hillary Clinton at Yale Law School." *The Hillary Clinton Quarterly*. March 31, 2009.

16 Amy Chozik, "How Hillary Clinton Went Undercover to Examine Race in Education." *The New York Times*, Dec. 27, 2015.

17 http://www.ontheissues.org/2016/Hillary_Clinton_Welfare_+_Poverty.htm Source: *The Inside Story*, by Judith Warner, p. 92, Aug 1, 1993

18 Tom Gerencer, "Hillary Clinton Net Worth." *Money Nation*. April 2, 2016.

19 Michelle Goldberg, "Can Hillary Clinton Win Over the Left?" *The Nation*, Aug. 25, 2015.

20 Tom Gerencer, "Hillary Clinton Net Worth." *Money Nation*. April 2, 2016.

21 Brian Ross, Maddy Sauer, Rhonda Schwartz, "Clinton Remained Silent as Wal-Mart Fought Unions." ABC News, Jan. 31, 2008. http://abcnews.go.com/Blotter/clinton-remained-silent-wal-mart-fought-unions/story?id=4218509

22 Ibid.

23 Hillary Rodham Clinton, *Living History*. Scribner, 2004. 246.

24 Paul Starr, "The Hillarycare Mythology." *The American Prospect*, Sept. 13, 2007.

25 Ibid.

26 Michelle Goldberg, "Can Hillary Clinton Win Over the Left?" *The Nation*, Aug. 25, 2015.

27 Paul Starr, "The Hillarycare Mythology." The American Prospect, Sept. 13, 2007.

28 Hillary Rodham Clinton, Living History. Scribner, 2004. 261.

29 Michelle Goldberg, "Can Hillary Clinton Win Over the Left?" *The Nation*, Aug. 25, 2015.

30 Ibid.

31 "What Is Hillary's Greatest Accomplishment?" *Politico Magazine*. Sept. 17, 2015.

32 Paul Starr, "The Hillarycare Mythology." *The American Prospect*, Sept. 13, 2007.

33 Jonathan Allen, Amie Parnes. *HRC: State Secrets and the Rebirth of Hillary Clinton*. Broadway Books, 2015, 176.

34 James Passeri, "Valeant Parries Clinton Attack with Defense of Drug Prices." *Real Money*, March 1, 2016.

35 Paul Starr, "The Hillarycare Mythology." *The American Prospect*, Sept. 13, 2007.

36 Michelle Alexander, "Why Hillary Clinton Doesn't Deserve the Black Vote." *The Nation*. Feb. 10, 2016.

37 Ibid.

38 Ibid.

39 Janell Ross, "Why Hillary Clinton's 'super-predator' concession is such a big moment for political protest." *The Washington Post*, Feb. 26, 2016.

40 Bryce Covert, "Hillary Wants to Help the Families at the Bottom. So Will She Change Her Mind About Welfare Reform?" *The Nation*, May 11, 2015.

41 Elise Foley, "Hillary Clinton Says She'll End Private Prisons, Stop Accepting Their Money." *Huffington Post*, Oct. 23, 2015.

42 https://www.hillaryclinton.com/issues/criminal-justice-reform/

43 Hillary Rodham Clinton, *Living History*. Scribner, 2004. 326.

44 Hillary Rodham Clinton, *Living History*. Scribner, 2004. 366.

45 Glenn Thrush, "Bill Clinton Swipes Back at Bernie Sanders on Welfare Reform." *Politico Magazine*. Feb. 25, 2016.

46 Ibid.

47 Bryce Covert, "Hillary Clinton Wants to Help Families at the Bottom. So Will She Change Her Mind About Welfare Reform?" *The Nation*, May 11, 2015.

48 H. Luke Shaefer, University of Michigan, and Kathryn Edin, Harvard University, "Rising Extreme Poverty in the United States and the Response of Federal Means-Tested Transfer Programs," National Poverty Center Working Paper #13-06, May 2013, National Poverty Center, http://www.thenation.com/wp-content/uploads/2015/05/2013-06-npc-working-paper.pdf

49 Nicola Smith, "Neoliberalism." *Encyclopedia Britannica*.

50 Arun Gupta, "How the Democrats Became the Party of Neoliberalism." *Counterpunch*. Nov. 3, 2014.

51 Michelle Goldberg, "Can Hillary Clinton Win Over the Left?" *The Nation*, Aug. 25, 2015.

52 Leroy Pelton, "Hillary Clinton's Family Values." *Jacobin Magazine*, June 16, 2015.

53 Hillary Rodham Clinton, *Living History*. Scribner, 2004. 291.

54 Mark Karlin, "How Hillary Clinton Betrayed the Children's Defense Fund for Political Gain." *Buzzflash*. Jan. 24, 2008.

55 Hillary Rodham Clinton, *Living History*. Scribner, 2004. 369.

56 Johanna Brenner, "The Promise of Socialist Feminism." *Jacobin Magazine*. Sept. 18, 2014.

57 Ibid.

58 Raymond Hernandez, "With a Step Right, Clinton Agitates the Left." *The New York Times*, May 22, 2002.

59 Ibid.

60 Andrew Stiles, "Analysis: Hillary Clinton vs. Bernie Sanders on Welfare Reform." *Washington Free Beacon*, July 23, 2015.

61 Leroy Pelton, "Hillary Clinton's Family Values." *Jacobin Magazine*, June 16, 2015.

62 Bryce Covert, "Hillary Clinton Wants to Help Families at the Bottom. So Will She Change Her Mind About Welfare Reform?" *The Nation*, May 11, 2015.

63 http://www.ontheissues.org/2016/Hillary_Clinton_Welfare_+_Poverty.htm

64 http://www.ontheissues.org/2016/Hillary_Clinton_Welfare_+_Poverty.htm Source: The Hyde Park Declaration 00-DLC3 on Aug 1, 2000

65 Kathleen Geier, Joan Walsh, Jamelle Bouie, Doug Henwood, Heather Digby Parton, Steven Teles, and Richard Yeleson, "Who's Ready for Hillary?" *The Nation*. Nov 24, 2014.

66 Ibid.

67 Sarah Ditum, "The Thatcher Problem." *The New Statesman*. Feb. 3, 2016.

68 Jay Newton-Small, "Exclusive: Hillary Clinton on Running and Governing as a Woman." *Time Magazine*. Jan. 7, 2016.

69 Hilary Moss, "Hillary Clinton & Angela Merkel Celebrate Shared Love of Pant Suits (PHOTOS)." *Huffington Post*, June 7, 2011.

70 Hillary Rodham Clinton, *Living History*. Scribner, 2004. 417-418.

71 Jim Waterson, Lynzy Billing, "House of Cards Creator: Hillary Clinton is the Real Claire Underwood." *Buzzfeed*. July 10, 2015.

72 Jessica Taylor, "New Clinton Spanish Posters: Hillary or Evita?" NPR.org, Oct. 15, 2015.

73 Jonathan Watts, "Berta Cáceres, Honduran Human Rights and Environment Activist, Murdered." *The Guardian*. March 4, 2016.

74 Camilla Mortensen, "Jill Stein, Green Party Candidate, Calls for Change." *Eugene Weekly.com*, Jan. 28, 2016.

75 Michelle Goldberg, "Hard Choices: I Used to Hate Hillary. Now I'm Voting for Her." *Slate*, Feb. 10, 2016.

76 Michelle Goldberg, "Hillary's Head." *Slate*. Nov. 12, 2015.

77 Chez Pazienza, "If You're Liberal and You Think Hillary Clinton is Corrupt and Untrustworthy, You're Rewarding 25 Years of GOP Smears." *TheDailyBanter.com*, Jan. 31, 2016.

78 Hannah Groch-Begley, "Media Return to Deriding Hillary Clinton's Laugh." *MediaMatters.org* Blog, Oct. 14, 2015.

79 Aviva Shen, "New York Post Goes After Hillary Clinton with Blatantly Sexist Cover." *ThinkProgress.org*, Jan. 24, 2013.

80 Jessica Valenti, " 'Don't Tell Her to Smile': The subtle sexism still facing Hillary Clinton." *The Guardian*. March 17, 2016.

81 Hillary Rodham Clinton, *Living History*. Scribner, 2004. 303-304.

82 Joan Walsh, "Why I'm Supporting Hillary Clinton, With Joy and Without Apologies," *The Nation*, Jan. 27, 2016.

83 Hana Schank, "My Gen-X Hillary Problem: I Know Why We Don't 'Like' Clinton." *Salon.com*, March 2, 2016.

84 Michelle Goldberg, "Hillary's Head." *Slate*. Nov. 12, 2015.

85 Rodolfo Mendoza-Denton, "Is Hillary Clinton Pathologically Ambitious?" *Psychology Today* Blog. Oct. 6, 2010.

86 Michelle Goldberg, "Hard Choices: I Used to Hate Hillary. Now I'm Voting for Her." *Slate*, Feb. 10, 2016.

87 Amanda Hess, "Bernie vs. Hillary." *Slate*. Feb 9, 2016.

88 Tim Murphy, "We're Not Crazy," *Mother Jones* Sept/Oct. 2015.

89 Rebecca Traister, "The Bernie Sanders' Sexist New Argument: Hillary Tries Too Hard." *NYMag.com*, April 7, 2016.

90 Keli Goff, "What Hillary Clinton Needs to Tell Voters Who Don't Want to Have a Beer With Her." *The Daily Beast.com*, March 26, 2016.

91 Michelle Goldberg, "Hard Choices: I Used to Hate Hillary. Now I'm Voting for Her." *Slate*, Feb. 10, 2016.

92 Ibid.

93 Anna March, "Even When Hillary Wins, She Loses." *Salon.com*, Feb. 2, 2016.

94 Jann S. Wenner, "Hillary Clinton for President." *Rolling Stone*. March 23, 2016.

95 Keli Goff, "What Hillary Clinton Needs to Tell Voters Who Don't Want to Have a Beer With Her." *The Daily Beast.com*, March 26, 2016.

96 S. A. Miller, "Bernie Sanders hits Hillary Clinton's 'evolution' on tough issues," *The Washington Times*, Nov. 8, 2015. http://www.washingtontimes.com/news/2015/nov/8/bernie-sanders-vermont-senator-hits-hillary-clinto/

97 Jocelyn Boryczka, *Suspect Citizens: Women, Virtue and Vice in Backlack Politics.* Temple University Press, 2012, p. 42.

98 Ibid., 161.

99 Scott Lemieux, "Hillary Clinton has evolved since the '90s. You probably have too." *The Week,* Feb. 3, 2016. http://theweek.com/articles/603127/hillary-clinton-evolved-since-90s-probably-have

100 John Harwood, "Biden Looks Back, Aspirations Intact." *The New York Times,* April 21, 2016.

101 "Fact Checkers Confirm Hillary Clinton is More Honest Than Any of Her 2016 Opponents." *DailyNewsBin.com*, March 20, 2016.

102 Jill Abramson, "This May Shock You: Hillary Clinton is Fundamentally Honest." *The Guardian*, March 28, 2016.

103 David Sherfinski, "Bernie Sanders surge reflects likability, not voter shift, analysts say." *The Washington Times*, Jan. 21, 2016.

104 Jann S. Wenner, "Hillary Clinton for President." *Rolling Stone.* March 23, 2016.

105 Joan Walsh, "Why I'm Supporting Hillary Clinton, With Joy and Without Apologies," *The Nation*, Jan. 27, 2016.

106 Amanda Hess, "Everyone is Wrong about the Bernie Bros." *Slate*, Feb. 3, 2016.

107 Joan Walsh, "Why I'm Supporting Hillary Clinton, With Joy and Without Apologies," *The Nation*, Jan. 27, 2016.

108 Sady Doyle, "More Than Likable Enough." *Slate*, Dec. 23, 2015.

109 Tom McCarthy, "Albright: 'special place in hell' for women who don't support Clinton." *The Guardian*, Feb. 6, 2016.

110 Maureen Dowd, "When Hillary Clinton Killed Feminism." *The New York Times*, Feb. 13, 2016.

111 Gloria Steinem, "March 22, 1998: Why Feminists Support Clinton." *The New York Times*, Sept. 25, 2010.

112 Amy Chozik, " '90s scandals threaten to erode Clinton's strength with women," *The New York Times*, Jan. 201, 2016.

113 Conor Friedersdorf, "Why Hillary Clinton Won't Pay for Disparaging Her Husband's Accusers." *The Atlantic*, Feb. 14, 2014.

114 Hillary Rodham Clinton. *Living History*. Scribner, 2004. Photos 61 and 62.

115 Lindsey Boerma, "Hillary Clinton Stands By Her Defense of 1975 Rape Suspect." *CBSNews.com*, July 8, 2014.

116 Maureen Dowd, "When Hillary Clinton Killed Feminism." *The New York Times*, Feb. 13, 2016.

117 Ava Vidal, " 'Intersectional Feminism'. What the hell is it? (and why you should care)" *The Telegraph*, Jan. 15, 2014.

118 Clare Foran, "Hillary Clinton's Intersectional Politics." *The Atlantic*, March 9, 2016.

119 Cynthia Weber, "Is Bernie Sanders a Better Feminist than Hillary Clinton?" *Newsweek*, Feb. 14, 2016.

120 "Hillary Clinton's farcically late conversion on gay marriage." *The Economist.com* blog, March 18, 2013.

121 https://en.wikipedia.org/wiki/Women%27s_Rights_Are_Human_Rights

122 Michelle Goldberg, "Can Hillary Clinton Win Over the Left?" *The Nation*, Aug. 25, 2015.

123 Hillary Rodham Clinton, *Hard Choices*. Simon & Schuster, 2015, 152.

124 Johanna Brenner, "The Promise of Socialist Feminism." *Jacobin Magazine*. Sept. 18, 2014.

125 http://correctrecord.org/hillary-clinton-a-fighter-for-equal-pay/

126 Michelle Goldberg, "Can Hillary Clinton Win Over the Left?" *The Nation*, Aug. 25, 2015.

127 Johanna Brenner, "The Promise of Socialist Feminism." *Jacobin Magazine*. Sept. 18, 2014.

128 Kathleen Geier, Joan Walsh, Jamelle Bouie, Doug Henwood, Heather Digby Parton, Steven Teles, and Richard Yeleson, "Who's Ready for Hillary?" *The Nation*. Nov 24, 2014.

129 Tom Gerencer, "Hillary Clinton Net Worth." *Money Nation*. April 2, 2016.

130 Daniel Gross, "How Hillary and Bill Clinton Parlayed Decades of Public Service into Vast Wealth," *Fortune*, Feb. 15, 2016.

131 Tom Gerencer, "Hillary Clinton Net Worth." *Money Nation*. April 2, 2016.

132 David Fahrenthold, Tom Hamburger, and Rosalind S. Helderman. "The inside story of how the Clintons built a $2 billion global empire." *The Washington Post*, June 2, 2015.

133 Ibid.

134 Jonathan Allen, Amie Parnes. *HRC: State Secrets and the Rebirth of Hillary Clinton. Broadway Books,* 2015. 276.

135 Zeke J. Miller, "Obama Completes His Slow About-Face on Super PACS." *Time Magazine*, Feb. 28, 2014.

136 Callum Borchers, "Hillary Clinton's Goldman Sachs speech transcripts are now a campaign issue. Why weren't they before?" *The Washington Post*. Feb. 5, 2016.

137 Chris Cillizza, "Why won't Clinton release the transcripts of those paid speeches?" *The Washington Post*, Feb. 7, 2016.

138 Jill Abramson, "This May Shock You: Hillary Clinton is Fundamentally Honest." *The Guardian,* March 28, 2016.

139 James V. Grimaldi, Rebecca Ballhaus. "UBS Deal Shows Clinton's Complicated Ties." *The Wall Street Journal*, July 30, 2015.

140 William D. Cohan, "A First-Person History Lesson From Robert Rubin.*" The New York Times*, Nov. 19, 2014.

141 http://www.state.gov/r/pa/prs/ps/2009/sept/129535.htm

142 Naomi Klein, "The Problem with Hillary Clinton isn't Just her Corporate Cash. It's Her Corporate Worldview." *The Nation*, April 6, 2016.

143 Matt Taibbi, "Hillary's Take on the Banks Won't Hold Up." *Rolling Stone*, Oct. 14, 2015.

144 Lauren Carroll, "Bill Clinton: Glass-Steagall Repeal Had Nothing to do with Financial Crisis". *Politifact.com*, Aug. 19, 2015 http://www.politifact.com/truth-o-meter/statements/2015/aug/19/bill-clinton/bill-clinton-glass-steagall-had-nothing-do-financi/

145 Lauren Carroll, "Hillary Clinton says she called for Wall Street regulations early in financial crisis," *Politifact.com*, July 15, 2015 http://www.politifact.com/truth-o-meter/statements/2015/jul/15/hillary-clinton/hillary-clinton-says-she-called-wall-street-regula/

146 Press release, American Presidency Project http://www.presidency.ucsb.edu/ws/?pid=96569

147 Amy Chozik, "Campaign Casts Hillary Clinton as the Populist It Insists She Has Always Been." *The New York Times*, April21, 2015.

148 Ibid.

149 Hillary Clinton, "My Plan to Prevent the Next Crash." *Bloomberg Review*, Oct. 8, 2015.

150 https://www.hillaryclinton.com/issues/plan-raise-american-incomes/

151 Thomas Piketty, "Thomas Piketty on the rise of Bernie Sanders: U.S. enters a new political era." *The Guardian*. Feb. 16, 2016.

152 Ibid.

153 Michael A. Memoli, "On a big day for minimum-wage laws, Hillary Clinton, not Bernie Sanders, grabs the spotlight." *The Los Angeles Times*, April 4, 2016.

154 Tami Luhby and Tiffany Baker, "What is Middle Class, Anyway?" *CNNMoney*, http://money.cnn.com/infographic/economy/what-is-middle-class-anyway/

155 Hillary Rodham Clinton, *Living History*. Scribner, 2004. 385.

156 http://www.biography.com/people/hillary-clinton-9251306#early-years

157 Zack Schwartz-Weinstein, "When Bill and Hillary Crossed the Picket Line." *Jacobin Magazine*, Feb. 13, 2016.

158 Brian Ross, Maddy Sauer, Rhonda Schwartz. "Clinton Remained Silent as Wal-Mart Fought Unions." *ABC News*, Jan. 31, 2008. http://abcnews.go.com/Blotter/clinton-remained-silent-wal-mart-fought-unions/story?id=4218509

159 Michelle Goldberg, "Can Hillary Clinton Win Over the Left?" *The Nation*, Aug. 25, 2015.

160 http://correctrecord.org/hillary-clinton-a-fighter-for-equal-pay/

161 Michelle Goldberg, "Can Hillary Clinton Win Over the Left?" *The Nation*, Aug. 25, 2015.

162 Jamiles Lartey, "Clinton meets with Nabisco factory workers facing imminent job cuts." *The Guardian*. March 14, 2016.

163 Jeanne Sahadi. "Hillary Clinton: Workers should get bigger piece of company profits." *CNNMoney.com*, July 14, 2015.

164 Michelle Goldberg, "Can Hillary Clinton Win Over the Left?" *The Nation*, Aug. 25, 2015.

165 Amy Chozik, "Campaign Casts Hillary Clinton as the Populist It Insists She Has Always Been." *The New York Times*, April 21, 2015.

166 David Sirota, "Cables Show Hillary Clinton's State Department Deeply Involved in Trans-Pacific Partnership." *International Business Times*, July 31, 2015.

167 Clark Mindock and David Sirota, "Panama Papers: Clinton, Obama Pushed Trade Deal Amid Warnings Warnings It Would Make Money Laundering, Tax Evasion Worse." *International Business Times*, April 4, 2016.

168 David Sirota, Andrew Perez, and Matthew Cunningham-Cook, "As Colombian Money Flowed to Clintons, State Department Took No Action to Prevent Labor Violations." *International Business Times*, April 8, 2015.

169 David Sirota, Andrew Perez, and Matthew Cunningham-Cook. "As Colombian Money Flowed to Clintons, State Department Took No Action to Prevent Labor Violations." *International Business Times,* April 8, 2015.

170 Emily Cadei, "Bernie Sanders and Hillary Clinton are More Alike Than You Think," *Newsweek*, Feb. 13, 2016.

171 Kathleen Geier, Joan Walsh, Jamelle Bouie, Doug Henwood, Heather Digby Parton, Steven Teles, and Richard Yeleson, "Who's Ready for Hillary?" *The Nation*. Nov 24, 2014.

172 Ibid.

173 Joan Walsh, "Why I'm Supporting Hillary Clinton, With Joy and Without Apologies," *The Nation*, Jan. 27, 2016.

174 Michelle Goldberg, "Can Hillary Clinton Win Over the Left?" *The Nation*, Aug. 25, 2015.

175 https://www.hillaryclinton.com/issues/k-12-education/

176 http://billmoyers.com/2014/03/28/public-education-who-are-the-corporate-reformers/

177 Liza Featherstone, "Why This Socialist Feminist is Not Voting for Hillary." *The Nation*, Jan. 5, 2016.

178 Hillary Rodham Clinton. *Living History*. Scribner, 2004. 427.

179 Ibid., 382.

180 Naomi Klein, "The Problem with Hillary Clinton isn't Just her Corporate Cash. It's Her Corporate Worldview." *The Nation*, April 6, 2016.

181 James Hohmann, "Analysis: Four Reasons Hillary Clinton Lost the Democratic Debate." *Portland Press Herald*, March 10, 2015.

182 Michelle Goldberg, "Can Hillary Clinton Win Over the Left?" *The Nation*, Aug. 25, 2015.

183 Mariah Blake, "How Hillary Clinton's State Department Sold Fracking to the World." *Mother Jones,* Sept/Oct. 2014. http://www.motherjones.com/environment/2014/09/hillary-clinton-fracking-shale-state-department-chevron

184 Alex Seitz-Wald, "Hillary Clinton (finally) comes out against Keystone Pipeline." *MSNBC.com*, Sept. 22, 2015.

185 https://www.hillaryclinton.com/briefing/factsheets/2016/02/12/hillary-clintons-plan-for-ensuring-safe-and-responsible-natural-gas-production/

186 Alex Emmons, "Hillary Clinton Wants to Regulate Fracking, But Still Accepts a Lot of Fracking Money.*" The Intercept.* March 9, 2016.

187 Rebecca Leber, "Hillary Clinton's Big Shift on Fracking," *Mother Jones*. March 7, 2016.

188 Dan Merica, "Hillary Clinton: Climate Change Has Contributed to Refugee Crisis, Including Syria." *CNN.com*, Nov. 4, 2015.

189 Amy Sherman, "Bernie Sanders says that Hillary Clinton opposed driver's licenses for illegal immigrants." *Politifact.com*, March 9, 2016 http://www.politifact.com/florida/statements/2016/mar/09/bernie-s/bernie-sanders-says-hillary-clinton-opposed-driver/

190 James Hohmann, "Analysis: Four Reasons Hillary Clinton Lost the Democratic Debate." *Portland Press Herald*, March 10, 2015.

191 Ajay Gupta, "Hillary Clinton's Immigration Policy Seeks to Erase Bill Clinton's Welfare Reform Legacy," *Forbes*, April 7, 2016.

192 https://www.hillaryclinton.com/issues/immigration-reform/

193 Ajay Gupta, "Hillary Clinton's Immigration Policy Seeks to Erase Bill Clinton's Welfare Reform Legacy," *Forbes*, April 7, 2016.

194 http://www.msnbc.com/shuttered

195 Irin Carmon, "Sanders dismisses major women's groups as 'establishment," MSNBC, Jan. 20, 2016 http://www.msnbc.com/msnbc/sanders-dismisses-major-womens-group-establishment

196 Joan Walsh, "Why I'm Supporting Hillary Clinton, With Joy and Without Apology," *The Nation*, Jan. 27, 2016.

197 Eesha Pandit, "Hillary Clinton's Game-Changer: Why her Call for Abandoning the Hyde Amendment is So Important." *Salon.com,* Jan. 15, 2016.

198 Illyse Hogue, "5 Reasons Why NARAL Pro-Choice America is Endorsing Hillary Clinton." *Medium.com*. https://medium.com/@Ilysehogue/5-reasons-why-naral-pro-choice-america-is-endorsing-hillary-clinton-our-champion-4dc7e9fb68bf#.flepragto

199 Jonathan Allen, Amie Parnes, *HRC: State Secrets and the Rebirth of Hillary Clinton*. Broadway Books, 2015, 373.

200 Tim Teeman, "Hillary Clinton Suddenly Has a Big Gay Problem." *Daily Beast*, March 11, 2016.

201 Ibid.

202 Mark Joseph Stern, "Bernie Sanders Claims He's a Longtime Champion of Marriage Equality. It's Just Not True." *Slate*, Oct. 5, 2015. http://www.slate.com/blogs/outward/2015/10/05/bernie_sanders_on_marriage_equality_he_s_no_longtime_champion.html

203 Jonathan Allen, Amie Parnes. *HRC: State Secrets and the Rebirth of Hillary Clinton.* Broadway Books, 2015, 372.

204 Tim Teeman, "Hillary Clinton Suddenly Has a Big Gay Problem." *The Daily Beast*, March 11, 2016.

205 Valerie Bauerlein, "Hillary Clinton Challenges the Gun Lobby." *The Wall Street Journal*, March 10, 2016.

206 Julie Bosman, "Clinton Portrays Herself as a Pro-Gun Churchgoer." *The New York Times*, April 12, 2008.

207 Patrick L. Smith, "As reckless as George W. Bush: Hillary Clinton helped create disorder in Iraq, Libya, Syria – and, scarier, doesn't seem to understand how." *Salon.com*, March 13, 2016.

208 Jonathan Allen, Amie Parnes, *HRC: State Secrets and the Rebirth of Hillary Clinton.* Broadway Books, 2015, 257.

209 Jo Becker and Scott Shane, "Hillary Clinton, 'Smart Power' and a Dictator's Fall," *The New York Times*, Feb. 27, 2016.

210 Ibid.

211 Michelle Goldberg, "Can Hillary Clinton Win Over the Left?" *The Nation*, Aug. 25, 2015.

212 Anatoly Lieven, A Hawk Named Hillary. *The Nation*, Nov. 25, 2014.

213 Catherine Putz, "What Might a Hillary Clinton Presidency Mean for Asia?" *The Diplomat*. April 13, 2015.

214 Jonathan Allen, Amie Parnes. *HRC: State Secrets and the Rebirth of Hillary Clinton.* Broadway Books, 2015, 327.

215 Alexander Main, "Hillary Clinton's Emails and the Honduras Coup." Center for Economic and Policy Research, Sept. 23, 2015. http://cepr.net/blogs/the-americas-blog/the-hillary-clinton-emails-and-honduras

216 Mark Weisbrot, "Hard choices: Hillary Clinton admits role in Honduran coup aftermath." *Al Jazeera America*, Sept. 29, 2014. http://america.aljazeera.com/opinions/2014/9/hillary-clinton-honduraslatinamericaforeignpolicy.html

217 Yamiche Alcindor, "High Hopes for Hillary Clinton, Then Disappointment in Haiti." *The New York Times*, March 14, 2016.

218 "Michel Martelly Can't Lead Haiti's Transition," (editorial) *The Miami Herald*, Jan. 30, 2016.

219 Hillary Rodham Clinton, *Hard Choices*. Simon & Schuster, 2015, 147.

220 Michael Crowley, "Hillary Clinton's Unapologetically Hawkish Record Faces 2016 Test." *Time Magazine*. Jan. 14, 2014.

221 Press Trust of India, "Hillary Clinton: Will Evaluate U.S. Troop Presence in Afghanistan if Elected." *India.com*, Feb. 5, 2016.

222 Jonathan Allen, Amie Parnes. *HRC: State Secrets and the Rebirth of Hillary Clinton.* Broadway Books, 2015, 268-269.

223 Hillary Rodham Clinton, *Hard Choices*. Simon & Schuster, 2015, 185.

224 Jonathan Allen, Amie Parnes. *HRC: State Secrets and the Rebirth of Hillary Clinton.* Broadway Books, 2015, 333.

225 http://gawker.com/at-aipac-clinton-attacks-one-race-baiting-demagogue-i-1766203007

226 "What Is Hillary's Greatest Accomplishment?" *Politico Magazine*. Sept. 17, 2015.

227 Michelle Goldberg, "Can Hillary Clinton Win Over the Left?" *The Nation*, Aug. 25, 2015.

228 David Sirota and Andrew Perez, "Clinton Foundation Donors Got Weapons Deals from Hillary Clinton's State Department." *International Business Times*, May 26, 2016.

229 Press Trust of India, "Hillary Clinton: Sending Troops to Iraq, Syria will be terrible mistake." *India.com*, Feb. 4, 2016.

230 Earl Ofari Hutchinson, "Sorting Out Fact from Fiction About Hillary's Iraq War Vote." *Huffington Post*, Feb. 9, 2016.

231 Jann S. Wenner, "Hillary Clinton for President." *Rolling Stone*. March 23, 2016.

232 Hillary Rodham Clinton, *Hard Choices*. Simon & Schuster, 2015, 134.

233 Ibid., 137.

234 James Hohmann, "Analysis: Four Reasons Hillary Clinton Lost the Democratic Debate." *Portland Press Herald*, March 10, 2015.

235 Con Coughlin, "David Cameron Did Make a Mess of Libya –That's Why Obama's Comments Must Really Hurt." *The Telegraph*, March 11, 2016.

236 Jo Becker and Scott Shane, "Hillary Clinton, 'Smart Power' and a Dictator's Fall," *The New York Times*, Feb. 27, 2016.

237 Jonathan Allen, Amie Parnes. *HRC: State Secrets and the Rebirth of Hillary Clinton.* Broadway Books, 2015, 357.

238 Scott Shane and Jo Becker, "A New Libya, with 'Very Little Time Left'", *The New York Times*, Feb. 27, 2016.

239 Jo Becker and Scott Shane, "Hillary Clinton, 'Smart Power' and a Dictator's Fall," *The New York Times*, Feb. 27, 2016.

240 Adam Johnson, "Hillary Clinton's insane plan for a no-fly zone." *Al Jazeera America*, aljazeera.com, Dec. 29, 2015.

241 Jeffrey Sachs, "Hillary is the Candidate of the War Machine." *Huffington Post*, Feb. 5, 2016.

242 Amy Chozik, David E. Sanger, "Hillary Clinton Goes Beyond President Obama in Plan to Defeat ISIS," *The New York Times*, Nov. 19, 2015.

243 Arnie Seipel, "Why Did Hillary Clinton Say the U.S. is 'Where We Need to Be' in Syria?" *NPR.org*, Dec. 20, 2015.

244 Ijeoma Oluo, "How Not to Be an Asshole This Election Season," *The Establishment*, April 6, 2016.

245 Jann S. Wenner, "Hillary Clinton for President." *Rolling Stone.* March 23, 2016.

246 Okla Elliot, *Bernie Sanders: The Essential Guide,* 108.

247 http://www.theroot.com/articles/news/2015/06/hillary_clinton_at_black_church_in_missouri_all_lives_matter.html

248 http://www.huffingtonpost.com/entry/black-lives-matter-hillary-clinton_us_56180c44e4b0e66ad4c7d9fa

249 Michelle Goldberg, "Can Hillary Clinton Win Over the Left?" *The Nation*, Aug. 25, 2015.

250 Hillary Rodham Clinton, *Hard Choices.* Simon & Schuster, 2015, 49.

251 Michelle Goldberg, "Can Hillary Clinton Win Over the Left?" *The Nation*, Aug. 25, 2015.

252 Johanna Brenner, "The Promise of Socialist Feminism." *Jacobin Magazine.* Sept. 18, 2014.

253 Ibid.

254 Kathleen Geier, Joan Walsh, Jamelle Bouie, Doug Henwood, Heather Digby Parton, Steven Teles, and Richard Yeleson, "Who's Ready for Hillary?" *The Nation*. Nov 24, 2014. *http://www.thenation.com/article/whos-ready-hillary/*

255 Hillary Rodham Clinton. *Living History*. Scribner, 2004. 397.

256 Ibid., 437.

EYEWEAR PUBLISHING

we are an independent press
based in London, England.
Emphasis is on excellent new
work, in poetry and prose. Our
range is international and our
aim is true. Look into some of the
most stylish books around today.

SQUINT BOOKS
JEREMY CORBYN – ACCIDENTAL HERO W STEPHEN GILBERT
BERNIE SANDERS – THE ESSENTIAL GUIDE OKLA ELLIOTT
ADELE – THE OTHER SIDE AMY MACKELDEN
DONALD TRUMP – THE RHETORIC OLIVER JONES
THE EVOLUTION OF HILLARY RODHAM CLINTON SONYA HUBER

EYEWEAR PROSE
SUMIA SUKKAR THE BOY FROM ALEPPO WHO PAINTED THE WAR
ALFRED CORN MIRANDA'S BOOK

EYEWEAR LITERARY CRITICISM
MARK FORD THIS DIALOGUE OF ONE - WINNER OF THE 2015 PEGASUS AWARD
FOR POETRY CRITICISM FROM THE POETRY FOUNDATION (CHICAGO, USA).

EYEWEAR POETRY
MORE THAN 30 TITLES

SEE **WWW.EYEWEARPUBLISHING.COM**